INSIDE THE
Trenches

INSIDE THE
Trenches

An Educator's Guide for What
You CAN DO in the Classroom

Adam Dovico

Cover design by Chrissi Major
ISBN: 1499570171
ISBN 13: 9781499570175

Table of Contents

Prologue ix

Introduction xv

Chapter 1: You CAN ... Be an Inspiration 1

Chapter 2: You CAN ... Do Whatever It Takes 5

Chapter 3: You CAN ... Lose Your Shame 11

Chapter 4: You CAN ... Connect With Your Students 16

Chapter 5: You CAN ... Be Lucky Sometimes 21

Chapter 6: You CAN ... Help Others 26

Chapter 7: You CAN ... Show Camaraderie 32

Chapter 8: You CAN ... Document Your Experiences 36

Chapter 9: You CAN ... Teach Manners 41

Chapter 10: You CAN ... Eat 46

Chapter 11: You CAN ... Press Reply 50

Chapter 12: You CAN ... Be a Storyteller 55

Chapter 13: You CAN ... Incentivize 60

Chapter 14: You CAN ... Suit Up 63

Chapter 15: You CAN ... Be Humbled 67

[Handwritten annotations:]
- _"1/9" next to Introduction_
- _Chapter 2: snake, Grocery store_
- _Chapter 3: dress up, be goofy_
- _Chapter 4: connect more, tracking_
- _"1/16" Chapter 5: Blessed with events that just click together_
- _Chapter 6: community service_
- _Chapter 7: cohesive team @ work, not dysfunctional_
- _Chapter 8: memorable quotes & moments with kids_
- _Chapter 10: snacks + foods from other cultures, cultural cook-out_
- _Chapter 11: stay caught up on emails & communication_
- _Chapter 12: weave story throughout lesson_
- _Chapter 13: incentives for motivation_
- _Chapter 14: Tuesday is for T.I.E.S. - dress up_
- _Chapter 15: think ahead about repercussions & evaluate decisions better_

Chapter 16: You CAN ... Utilize Your Resources *Krispy Kremes Parents come in to talk to kids* ... 71

11/30

Chapter 17: You CAN ... Visit Your Students' Homes. 77

Chapter 18: You CAN ... Be Clean and Organized 81

Chapter 19: You CAN ... Share Ideas. *with other teachers* 86
peer teach-

Chapter 20: You CAN ... Start a Club. *GNC* 90

Chapter 21: You CAN ... Be a Cheerleader. *Be encouraging* 94
"You can do it"

Chapter 22: You CAN ... Have Your Students Help You Propose 97

Chapter 23: You CAN ... Tell About the Good Ol' Days 101

Chapter 24: You CAN ... Tip Your Humpty 105

Chapter 25: You CAN ... Put Yourself in Your Students'

Shoes (or iPhones). 109

Chapter 26: You CAN ... Use Data. 116

Chapter 27: You CAN ... Learn in First Class 121

Chapter 28: You CAN ... Set the Pace 124

Chapter 29: You CAN ... Videotape Yourself. 129

Chapter 30: You CAN ... Create Mini-Me's 133

Chapter 31: You CAN ... Informally Assess. 138

Chapter 32: You CAN ... Show Appreciation Towards Each Other . . . 144

Chapter 33: You CAN ... Correct Behaviors Immediately. 147

Chapter 34: You CAN ... Teach Outside Your Comfort Zone. 151

Chapter 35: You CAN ... Learn Names. 157

Chapter 36: You CAN ... Pay It Forward 162

Chapter 37: You CAN ... Be Inside the Trenches. 167

About the Author 171

Stay Connected!. 173

Dedication

To Mom and Dad for being my first teachers.
To Marc for being my first student.
To Mr. Bruns for being a mentor.
To all of my students for being my motivation.
To Jaclyn and Ryder for being my inspiration.

Prologue

When I was about five years old, I knew exactly what I wanted to be when I grew up. I told my parents, my brother, and anyone else who would listen. I wrote a letter to the CEO of the company, I prepared my uniform, and even practiced what I was going to do when I began working there.

First, let me paint a picture for you. Today I stand at an average 5'10" and weigh in at the super light-weight qualifying limit of 140 pounds. I was in the 10th percentile in weight from the day I was born. I come from a long line of pasty-white New Jerseyans who would rather eat bagels and pizza than go to the gym. I can't stand fights—I've never been in one in my life. If I were a hockey player, I would likely win the Lady Byng Trophy (player with the most sportsmanship and gentlemanly conduct). Combine all of this and my dream of becoming *a professional wrestler* seems just a little bit ridiculous, doesn't it?

You see, I am a child of the 80's and Hulk Hogan was everything little kids wanted to be back then. Twenty-first century Hulk Hogan got a bit more suspect. Of course, The Ultimate Warrior and Andre the Giant were pretty awesome, too, back then, but The Hulkster was my hero. I begged my mom to let me become a professional wrestler and she agreed, though I look back now with a bit of skepticism as to her confidence in me.

The Shooting Star had high aspirations of becoming the champ!

The wrestling career went through phases over my early school years, which also included hopes of being a magician, basketball player, carpenter, photographer, and snake handler (more on that last one later).

When I was about ten years old, wanting to be a wrestler was hot and heavy in my mind again. My parents allowed me to sign up for "real" wrestling lessons so I could see what it felt like getting my head bashed into a mat.

It doesn't feel good. I promise.

I participated in my first tournament in my wrestling "career" after practicing for about two weeks. I wrestled in the 89-pound weight class. There were four ten-year-olds in my bracket and one of the kids did not show up. After I lost my opening match as a result of a pin with only thirteen seconds to go, there was no one to wrestle in my second match. Long story short, I "earned" third place and got a neat little bronze medal that I held onto for many years.

I managed to throw out my shoulder during the match, and with that injury, I ended my illustrious wrestling career, or at least for the moment. I realized years later that while I may not be equipped to wrestle with 6'7" 300-pound monsters, I could incorporate my passion for professional wrestling into what would become my true career, teaching.

Teaching for many years in North Carolina, I learned that professional "rasslin" is quite popular with the Southern folk. Ric Flair—WOOOOOOOOOO!—is a legend in the state, and I realized that many of my students (and their families) knew all about the current Superstars that are performing today. John Cena and The Rock are this generation's Hulk Hogan. After a few years of seeing this pattern, I began to realize that I could hook my students by incorporating wrestling themes or phrases into my teaching.

For instance, there is a World Wrestling Entertainment (WWE) Superstar named The Miz. Some of you reality television show connoisseurs may remember him as Mike Mizanin from MTV's *The Real World*. When he was on the show, he had a split persona where he became this "Miz" character and would talk and act like a wrestler while around the others in the house. Years later, he was able to make his dream come true by becoming a professional wrestler in the WWE. He is known for his cockiness and ego, and he has a catchphrase that goes "I'm the Miz, and I'm AWESOME!" Now when he says awesome, it's not just a spoken word, it is a proclamation of self-centeredness with passion and attitude.

I decided that since many of my students knew who he was, and his catchphrase is fun to say, I was going to incorporate this into my teaching. I explained to the students that when one of their classmates gives a stellar answer or demonstrates excellence, we would celebrate them with the AWESOME chant. For instance, if Shawl got a great answer, I would say to the class, "That's Shawl, and he's," and the class would all come in to join me with "AWWWWESOME!"

While the catchphrases are fun, I wanted to have a symbol of awesomeness, as well, that my students could be proud of. In my social studies class, there was a strong emphasis on being able to argue and defend your stance when we learned about various issues. Each week, we would have formal debates on current event topics, such as troop withdrawal from war zones, legalization of gay marriage, ethical use of the internet, and many more.

After the students debated, I would award the "World Debate Champion" of the week. At Wal-Mart, they sell replica WWE Championship belts. The debate champion for that week was awarded the belt and was permitted to wear it the entire week around school. Many of them even wore it to physical education class! They would also get their picture on my wall of debate champions. When other students and staff saw a child wearing the belt after coming out of my class, they knew what it meant. As a result, that child was uplifted, celebrated, and congratulated on his or her accomplishment.

Imani posing with her Debate Championship.

The other thing I took away from watching these super-human athletes on television was their confidence and passion. When they go through the curtain, they are in front of thousands of people all looking at them. If these men and women simply walked to the ring like they were walking down the street, the crowd would not have a connection to them. If they did not have passion or charisma, they would not be believable. I see myself in a similar role when I teach. While it is only thirty students in front of me, rather than ten thousand fans, I believe that with the same energy and passion for what I am doing, I am engaging my students. Once they are hooked, teaching my content becomes much easier.

While I may not personally be able to step inside of a ring and wrestle the likes of John Cena and The Rock, I realized that I *could* bring ideas from the wrestling world into my classroom that would engage, celebrate, and uplift my students. And that to me is … AWWWWWESOME!

Introduction

Throughout my teaching career I have been fortunate to have worked for many principals who have supported my wild ideas and sometimes unique requests. I have also worked with fantastic adults who have accompanied me on amazing journeys. But there are also some who have not always believed in me; some who looked at me with rolling eyes when I wanted to take on fanatical ventures. It did not offend me, but rather it saddened me. It saddened me because that teacher's students were not going to experience something different, something unique.

While teaching fifth grade years ago at an inner-city school, I thought it would be fun to build eco-columns during the ecosystem unit in science. It involves cutting up two-liter soda bottles and joining them together in order to make a terrarium and aquarium all-in-one contraption. The kids grow plants, add animals, and watch nature right in front of them take course. It's a project that takes preparation and organization, but in the end, the kids love it and it provides a wealth of content to discuss. I had done it for several years prior at previous schools. In this school, though, the team decided it was something we could not do. We did not have the money, time, or resources to make it happen. I offered to get everything prepared, but they still were not on board.

In the end, we didn't do it, and I regret that I didn't push harder to make it happen. The students, particularly this group who could have truly benefitted from this project, missed out on something special. This type of attitude exists in many schools across the country, and it's disheartening that so many students are missing out on valuable real-life learning opportunities because their teachers believe something is not possible.

For several years, I worked at a school called the Ron Clark Academy in Atlanta, Georgia. The school, founded by Disney Teachers of the Year Ron Clark and Kimberly Bearden, was built to be different. Be bold. Be unique. They surrounded themselves with teachers who believed anything could happen, and in fact, made things happen.

Ron's motto, quite appropriately, is "make it happen." He has explained in his books (*The Essential 55, The Excellent 11, The End of Molasses Classes*) how he has made things happen in his career, including the daunting task of building this school from scratch. The school serves a dual purpose: to educate its fifth- through eighth-grade children, but also to open its doors to educators from around the world so that they may look inside of its classrooms and take back strategies that they may use in their teaching.

Having been observed and conducted professional development for over 10,000 educators, I have heard every excuse in the book for why something cannot be done. *"We don't have those kids. We don't have the money. My kids can't do that. I don't have the time. My administration would never let me do that. I don't have any parent support."* After a while, I truly do wonder if *anything* can be done. But then I hear another group of teachers talk about how they are going to take the House System that the Ron Clark Academy uses (a la Harry Potter) and make it work in their school. Or I hear about how teachers are going to work together to create a quiz bowl at their school, with local media to cover the event. That's the "make it happen" attitude that separates the pack.

This positive, make it happen attitude, carries on to the students who believe that they can make anything happen. When you have an entire school who believes, who cares, who is driven to find results, magic happens. There are road blocks along the way, there are naysayers you will face, but in the end, the desire to find what you *can* do proves itself.

This book is about discussing what you can do first as an educator, but truly, what you can accomplish in your life when you believe in your goals.

I will share stories from my own personal teaching career, but also take tales from co-workers and friends I have met along the way. You will hear about extraordinary individuals from across the country, who I have been able to observe in the classroom, who make magic happen each day. And as you will see, magic is not always that complicated to pull off when you suspend disbelief!

As you read, it is not about doing each of these things presented. But rather, these tales should be symbolic to you, inspiring ideas that can translate into your own teaching or life. Take them, make them your own, and provide amazing opportunities to your students.

Before we begin, I want to tell about a moving speech I recently heard that had a message that has made me think deeply about my mission in life. In one of my roles with the Ron Clark Academy (RCA), I was in charge of the on-site training division of the school. I traveled the country, providing continuing professional development at schools after they had been through the training at RCA.

I had a few school trainings in a row where I was beginning to get down on myself because it just seemed that the school staffs I was speaking to were not letting the words sink in. They were quick to dismiss ideas and cynical with anything that might change the status quo.

Well, I just happened to be conducting training in Atlanta, and I stopped by RCA to say hi to my co-workers and kids after school. I had been planning on simply stopping by for a minute and then heading to the hotel after some greetings. One of my good friends, Gina Coss, asked if I wanted to go to a Women's HerStory Event called Ubuntu (a South African philosophy used to describe the interconnectedness of all women and girls) held by the National Center for Civil and Human Rights. I admittedly was tired and a bit tentative since it was an all-women's event, but I agreed to go with her and six of our female students.

At the event was a panel of four inspirational female change-makers, speaking about their experiences and motivation in making societal change. One of the speakers was Georgia Representative Stacey Abrams. Ms. Abrams is the first female minority leader for either party in the

Georgia Legislature. As she spoke, she had numerous exceptional pieces of guidance for the audience, but one of her phrases stuck out to me. In fact, I thought about it throughout the night and made connections to my own struggles I was facing at the time.

Ms. Abrams stated that in her job and in her life, she has to face people who do not always agree with her. To find that middle ground, to make people listen, she has learned that her approach has become "to convince, not convert."

She went on to explain that as Minority Leader in the House, she realized quickly that she was going to go into work each day and lose. When voting on bills and budgets, rarely is the minority going to win. So instead of becoming crestfallen or giving up, she redefined what success looked like. Success did not have to mean getting her bill passed. One definition of success was to convince representatives across party lines of her point of view. Make them think about issues from a different perspective. From there, she realizes she may not convert them, but she may be able to convince them to think differently.

As I thought about her words in relation to my job as a teacher trainer, but also a teacher, I realized my goal should be to create new fields of thought for educators; generate discussions and ideas that allow students to think from different points of view. In the end, I may not have converted anyone to my way of thinking, but if I made them think, convinced them that there are other ways to look at things, that can be considered a success.

Passion

Make it happen!

1.
You CAN ...
Be an Inspiration.

For several years my wife was an investment banker for a major US bank. She made good money and there were numerous perks. We used to go out with her co-workers, and it was not uncommon for them to drop $200 just at dinner. As a teacher, I was shuddering thinking of the very thought of that!

After several years, though, she realized it just was not for her. She was coming home dissatisfied and frustrated. It was taking a toll on us as a couple. I wanted to help her and be there for her, but it was becoming more difficult each day. Upon digging deeper in conversation to figure out what the issue was, she realized she was not, in her words, "helping people." There was no personal satisfaction from her job, and that was a problem for her.

You see, my wife, Jaclyn, has had hurdles she has had to overcome throughout her life that few people know about. When she was in middle school, her father was killed in an airplane that crashed outside of Pittsburgh, her hometown. Her mother, brother, and she mourned and struggled through the loss. But just a year and a half after she lost her father, her mother became ill with flu-like symptoms. When the problem persisted, she was hospitalized. Just a few short days later, she passed away as well.

Losing both of your parents in two years is not something any child should go through. As if the peer-pressure and cattiness of middle school isn't enough for the normal child to go through, Jaclyn was dealing with an additional burden that still sits with her today. As she went through middle school, she faced students who ranged from trying to say the right things to her, to downright being mean and inhumane. There was one girl who left a note in her locker that said her parents deserved to die. Wow!

Through it all, Jaclyn told me that there was one thing that kept her head above water, and that was her academics. It was the one thing she had control of in her life. As she went through high school and into college, she was consistently an honor-roll student, and graduated from Wake Forest University *Magna Cum Laude*.

My wife remains an inspiration to me because the few hurdles I have had to jump in my life are nothing in comparison to what she has had to do. She has overcome great tragedy and achieved at levels that most never dream of. If that cannot inspire you to work harder, I don't know what can.

I take the inspiration that Jaclyn gives to me and try to spread that to my students. While I do not have a poignant personal story necessarily to inspire them the way my wife does, I try to inspire through my actions, a good work ethic, and building relationships with my students and their families.

One of the tricky parts about teaching, especially in the elementary and middle school level, is that once your students move on, you often do not see what becomes of them. Do they find success? Are they safe, healthy, happy? In my office at home, I keep a row of pictures of all of my classes over the years, and sometimes I'll wonder what they are doing now. Are they still the same kid as when they were ten years old? Do they still have some of the same habits? Do they still talk to inanimate objects?

Luckily, technology has helped with this challenge. Many of my former students have found me on Facebook, and so they can send greetings along once in a while and check in. I received a private message from one of my former students, Devin. I had her in my first ever class. She was a sweet and caring girl and someone who you truly enjoy having in class. I had congratulated her on graduating high school and this is the message I received back:

"Mr. Dovico!!! Oh my goodness it's so nice hearing from you! Thank you! I can't believe I have already graduated high school. For the first couple years of college I will be going to Forsyth Tech Community College and then I'm going to transfer to a four year college. I'm not exactly sure what I'm going to major in yet, but I have strongly considered being an elementary school teacher because of how great of a teacher you were. My fifth grade year was honestly one of the best years I had, mainly because of you. And I think it would be so amazing if I could be able to have that effect on a child's life. Thank you again for everything!"

I am not a very emotional person, but this message brought a tear to my eye because this is the message that every teacher dreams of receiving. Hearing that you made an impact on your student's life, even eight years later, is an extraordinary feeling. Not to mention the fact that she is thinking of becoming a teacher—icing on the cake!

Reading this note from Devin made me think about another inspiration in my life, and the reason I became a teacher myself, Mr. Roy Bruns, my fifth-grade teacher at Demarest Elementary. Mr. Bruns is a towering 6'4", and as a fifth grader, that seemed more like 8'4". His voice was deep and he had giant hands that would point his index finger at you when he wanted to get his point across.

Sure, we learned our states and capitals and did grammar that year, but the content in fifth grade is not what I remember most about Mr. Bruns. This is the teacher who came to all of our Saturday basketball games and cheered us on. (Go Demarest Elementary School—undefeated my sixth grade year!) This is the man who drove me home when it was snowing a foot and a half since he lived near me. He took me out to lunch and talked to me about sports. As I went to middle school, he wrote recommendations for me for various contests. He was simply just a person who dedicated his life to his students.

He taught thousands of students over the years and earned the respect from colleagues and the town (he was also active in numerous sports and clubs). A couple of years ago his wife passed away. Unfortunately, I was not able to fly up to New Jersey to be at the funeral, but my brother, who also had him as a teacher, said that there were hundreds of former students and families there paying their respects. That shows the impact and influences that Mr. Bruns had on his students.

As I was thinking about why I wanted to be a teacher, what was the turning point that solidified this career path, it always went back to Mr. Bruns and the influence he had on me. I can honestly say that it is because of Mr. Bruns that I am a teacher, and the dedication and care he showed toward his students is something that I have taken with me to my classroom in my career.

So you may be wondering what happened with my wife? Jaclyn decided to leave the banking industry and pursue a completely different career path in the medical field as a doctor. Since she had been a business major in college, she had to get pre-med requirements in order to apply to medical school. She spent two years going back to school taking fun and easy courses, like organic chemistry I & II, biochem, and human physiology. Ok, well maybe fun and easy are not the right adjectives here, but in typical Jaclyn form, she worked her tail off and earned herself a 4.0 GPA in her courses.

As I write this, she is in medical school and loving every minute of it. The material is extremely challenging and complex, but I am seeing a new person. She is happy going to school each day, excited about learning science, and in general, eager to once again positively inspire those around her to be better people.

What CAN you do? You can be an inspiration in a child's life. You may not know the impact you have on that individual right away, but imprinting the values of hard work, passion, and care are things you can do right now to develop future successful citizens and professionals. You never know who you will inspire day to day, so make it a point to be your best and give it your all in whatever you do.

2.
You CAN ...
Do Whatever It Takes

Look, there are days when you don't want to get out of bed. The weather is cold, you had a late night, and you have a meeting with that parent who you just don't want to meet with. We've all been there. Everyone has bad days, rough spells, and their share of headaches, so what are you going to do to fix it?

I was finding myself in my second year of teaching having those types of days more often than not. As a young teacher, I knew that wasn't good. I had just come off of my first year of teaching, with a fairly energetic and quirky class, and entered year two with a class that simply wasn't the first. It wasn't their fault. There was nothing inherently wrong with them, but I just wasn't having the fun that I had like the year before.

It was around Christmastime when I decided something had to be done. I needed something to perk up the class, but more so, give myself a shot in the arm. I thought about changing the theme of my room from the black and gold of my alma mater, Wake Forest University (those poor Duke and Carolina fans in my room), but that wasn't going to cut it. I considered

5-25
chp 2,3,4,5

doing a few theme days, but those would come and go. Then I thought about what did I want more than anything when I was ten years old in fifth grade?

Remember in the beginning of the book when I told you about my various career dreams that came and went—the magician, basketball player, carpenter, photographer ... and snake handler. Well, one of those popped in my head as I was thinking about what to do with this class. You guessed it.

Ah yes, the snake handler. You see, I spent the majority of my nines and tens begging my mother to let me have a snake in the house. I had once whined and cried for a dog, but my mother, being fairly textbook obsessive compulsive, would not fathom the thought of a dog running around the house. When my brother and I were younger, we used to have to strip down to our underwear in the laundry room after soccer games before getting into the shower because dirt might track into the house. A dog simply wasn't going to happen.

So we had a fair share of more contained animals—fish, hermit crabs, iguanas, and even a sand lizard who we only kept for three days because in that time we only saw it once. They don't call it a sand lizard for nothing. Eventually, I decided that a snake would be the next logical progression in this hierarchy of pets. I had my mom partially convinced that we could get a snake; that is until we went to the pet store. We were hoping to find a snake that eats fruit or vegetables. We would have even settled on small insects. Unfortunately, Mother Nature didn't quite work that into snakes' diets. Mice, rats, rabbits, and other small fuzzy things were the only food that we saw that the snakes ate.

Needless to say, mom did not want even the thought of a mouse to exist in the house. The snake phase vanished at that point. Or so I thought!

Meet Deacon. Deacon is a four-and-a-half-foot ball python, appropriately named after the black and gold colors of Wake Forest University.

Deacon, the ball python snake.

Deacon was welcomed in a grand fashion to the class. After school one day, I went to a local exotic pet store in town. I bought him, the cage, heat lamps, and brought it all back to school when no one was there. I set everything up and put a sheet over the cage. The next day when the kids came in, I explained that they had a new classmate. He is a bit on the quiet side, but he'll be friends with you all in no time.

I proceeded to walk to the back of the room and ripped the sheet off the cage. What came next was a chorused mix of screams, "Cool," and utter fright. Diamond ran out of the room. Dustin was already asking to hold him. And Hannah was just staring at it like she couldn't believe there was a snake in the room.

It certainly did not take long for teachers and other kids around the school to learn about Deacon. If there is such a thing as a celebrity pet, this was it. I literally had random students in my room each day asking to see him. My room was the first door from the bus drop-off, so many students would somehow meander into my room to catch a glimpse of the snake before I would rush them off to their homeroom. Classes would take "field trips" to my room during my planning period to look at him. I believe Deacon for a short while became the most talked about thing at the school.

But then there was Mr. Jones, our lead custodian. Mr. Jones had been at the school for a long time, a really long time. With his Southern accent and mesh baseball hat, Mr. Jones could often be found cleaning the same floor tile for hours at a time. Whatever tile he picked that day, it would be the shiniest tile in the school. Unfortunately, the other tiles had to wait their day to be cleaned.

Mr. Jones was not as fond of the snake as the kids were. In fact, it took him weeks before he would even come into my classroom to empty the trash. I had to put my trashcan outside of the room if I wanted it emptied. Being around 23 years old at the time, I still had some prank tendencies in me, so I fully took advantage of this situation and made the most of it.

One of the other teachers gave me a rubber snake to have Deacon play with—though we found out snakes don't exactly play with toys like dogs do. So one day I told my kids to follow me quietly down the hall. We were going to have fun with this rubber snake. We tiptoed down the hallway to where Mr. Jones's office was. I had all of the kids line up against the wall. I knocked on his door. When it began to open, I had all the kids scream, and I held the rubber snake right up in front of his face. He screamed, slammed the door, and rumor has it he wet his pants.

Mr. Jones was a good sport about it and later got brave enough to even pet Deacon. Looking back, I'm lucky I didn't give the poor man a heart attack! I ended up having Deacon for about eight years in my classrooms, but after I had my son, I decided I needed to spend my time focusing on raising a child, not a snake anymore. My co-worker, Mr. Townsel, science teacher at the Ron Clark Academy, was gracious enough to take him and provide him a magnificent home in his classroom. Now, thousands of educators get to meet Deacon as they go through the Ron Clark Academy and his classroom.

Buying Deacon was symbolic for me. It meant having the chance to live out one of my childhood dreams of being a snake handler. But getting that snake also meant doing whatever it took to make a change in my life and in my classroom. I was tired of being tired. I wanted to have that excitement and fun that I experienced my first year with this class, as well. For me, getting Deacon was my way of getting things to where I wanted them to be.

As I traveled around the country, observing classrooms that had been livened up by a teacher's influence and seeing many that needed resuscitation, one gem in particular stands out in my mind. I was at an elementary school in rural North Carolina and did a quick tour with the principal before my observations began. She took me into a special education room just to see what this inventive teacher had created in her classroom.

What I walked into was a classroom-sized grocery store. I'm not talking about a bookshelf that she put some fake plastic food and a few boxes in. This was a legitimate transformation that time and thought went into. Shelf after shelf, aisle after aisle, boxes, cartons, and containers of food (most of which were empty) were neatly organized and labeled just as you would see in your local grocery store. While her room was only about half the size of a normal classroom I would see, she perfectly utilized her space to ensure that learning could take place in this real world setting.

Her students with learning differences were ascertaining real life skills and application of learning via a place that they were all familiar with. The principal told me that they role play jobs, practice social interactions, and discover how learning applies to your everyday life. The grocery store is used throughout the year in many of her lessons, and it has become a staple in not only her classroom, but a tool for teachers throughout the school to make use of.

Can you imagine trying to teach your students persuasive writing, but instead of just asking them to write an essay, they have to pick a food item from the store and create a commercial for it. When you are teaching markup and discount, what if students had to determine how much they could change the price so that you would still make a profit. In science, the students can look at the ingredients, measurements, and chemicals that go into the foods we eat. As you are doing all of this teaching, you can be teaching students how to greet customers, handle money, and be a responsible employee.

The possibilities for learning application are endless in this classroom, but this teacher clearly proved doing whatever it takes for your students can yield amazing results!

What CAN you do? You certainly don't need to buy a snake, especially if you are like Mr. Jones and deathly afraid of them. Deacon is a metaphor for going beyond the norm, thinking outside of the box, and doing whatever it takes to make the changes you want to make. For me, it was regaining the fun and excitement I had the year before. For you, it might be creating a grocery store or some other incredible undertaking. But don't be afraid to do something bold. Be different. Which leads us to our next chapter ...

3.
You CAN ...
Lose Your Shame

People have described my demeanor as "chill," "laid back," "calm," and other similar descriptors. My wife and I laugh because when our son was a baby, we are fairly certain he inherited my personality. When a million things were going on around him, he was as mellow as a mushroom, just sitting there taking it all in. He never got anxious or antsy; he just let whatever was happening happen. But then he turned two and he changed into my wife. That's another story.

I can't argue with that description of me. I would like to think I'm a fairly composed person. I tend not to get frazzled by tense situations, and I do my best to remain unruffled in the midst of craziness. With all that being said, having a calm personality is not an excuse for not having excitement and passion in your teaching. When I am in front of my students, or in front of an audience, I like to have fun. I do have a wry sense of humor (which is why I typically teach older grades), and I am not afraid to make a fool of myself, something that I have found is valuable in getting buy-in from my students.

I was blessed with the talent of being tone deaf. I come from a long line of ghastly singers, so bad that when my wife and I play *Rock Band* on our Nintendo Wii, we have to put it on "No Fail Mode" simply so the game doesn't end immediately with me singing. I have failed out of even the easiest songs they have in the game on the "Easy" play mode. They make those types of accommodations typically for seven-year-olds so they can boost their self-esteem while learning to read lyrics … and me. I would like to add I am a beast on guitar, though, so I am not completely useless in the game.

This handicap of horrifying crooning is nothing new. When I was in third grade, my music teacher, Mr. Anderson, had us go around the room and "sing" our name. In my head I sounded just fine as I joyfully sung A-dam Do-vi-co. A couple of weeks later was our school's winter musical. About five of us in the class were "awarded" a special job during the songs where we would blow across a two-liter bottle with water in it to make a whistling sound. I felt great! I got *the special job!* I was a straight A student, so I figured they needed some strong scholars to blow blissfully across these bottles so it was done correctly. As I grew older, and began to become self-aware of my vocal reality, I remembered back to my special job and realized it was meant for special people—who could not sing.

My insecurities as a singer continued throughout most of my high school and college years. Though, I admit, there were times in college when belting out "Living on a Prayer" at the top of my lungs with fellow New Jerseyans in Freddy B's might have happened. It took until I entered the classroom as a teacher to begin to realize that much like me as a child, most of my kids had no idea what good singing was. As I belted out songs that I wrote to go along with my content, they couldn't tell if it was Mr. Dovico or Justin Timberlake singing.

Of course, once you start singing, you've got to bust a move in there, as well. So here came the dancing to go right along with the singing. Now, unlike my singing, my dancing is not that bad, especially as they say, "for a white guy." I can pretend to "beef it up," "do the Dougie," and "the NaeNae," with the best of them. Nonetheless, a teacher singing, dancing, looking kind of odd up in front of the class is something that kids are going to laugh at. *And that's exactly what I want them to do!*

When the kids are laughing, having a good time, that means I have gotten their attention. Once I have their attention, the rest is a piece of cake. With buy-in comes listening ears, which allows me to teach my content. Even if the content is not particularly exciting, the engagement has already been established through a song, a dance, or something goofy. Like they say in tennis, "Advantage, teacher."

A few years ago, I was teaching my fifth graders about the 1950s and 1960s. I had my content all set and I taught my first lesson. It bombed. The kids weren't interested, and quite frankly, I wasn't interested. It just wasn't engaging enough. That afternoon, I drove out to a local costume store and rented a jumpsuit. Not just any jumpsuit, but The King's jumpsuit. The next day I came into class dressed in full Elvis gear. Mind you, it is nearing the summertime in Atlanta, and I am wearing a polyester costume. I was sweating from head to toe.

I went into my classroom and explained that Elvis had risen from the ground and was going to teach them about the good ol' days of rock n' roll. I spoke in my best Elvis voice, did a few dance moves, and signed some autographs. We had a good time, but more importantly, the kids were engaged, I was engaged, and the content seemed more meaningful (even though it was what I was going to teach anyway). We watched some clips of *Forrest Gump*, had great discussions on desegregation, and managed to learn a lot about the music of that era and its impact on society.

"The King" returned for a one-day appearance.

The kids in that class still remember that day and ask if Elvis is making a return. I tell them you can find him in Vegas in a few more years.

How many of you would be embarrassed to wear that outfit in front of your kids? How many of you would be uncomfortable singing and dancing in front of your students? If you answered yes to either of those, think about why. It is likely because of personal insecurities. Something you *can* do this year is challenge yourself to go beyond those insecurities and lose your shame. Go ahead, do something silly, make the kids laugh. I promise you they'll remember it. And so will you.

One of my dear friends and a phenomenal social studies teacher, Sarah Hildebrand, is a master at the art of the costume. I cannot even recall how many times she has dressed up over the years while working with her, but she manages to come up with the best outfits for her lessons.

Sarah's costumes not only bring her teaching to life, but it is giving the students something to remember her lessons by. It is not uncommon for a student to associate the content with a costume she was wearing. "Yeah, remember when Ms. Hildebrand was dressed up like in the soldier; that was when the East Berliners were trying to escape from the Communist side and sneak across to the West." How cool is it that just by wearing that costume, she is helping the students learn and appreciate (as opposed to memorizing) the content.

My personal favorite outfit Sarah has donned is a grandmother garb that she wears when she teaches about Maori (tribe from New Zealand) oral history and how the elders pass on the traditions and history of their people. I have seen where the kids are curious as to whether the person is actually a guest at the school or is Ms. Hildebrand! The costume she wears just adds to the engagement and buy-in factor for the kids, adding to the experience she is creating for the students.

What CAN you do? Bring your content to life! Dress up as a character from a book, write a song about something you're learning about, dye your hair some crazy color. Do whatever it takes to engage your students. If the only reason you are not doing something is because it makes you uncomfortable, what a great opportunity to teach your students a lesson in pushing beyond your safe zone.

Growth Mindset
outside of the box

4.
You CAN ...
Connect With Your Students

As you have probably learned by now, I am a proud alumnus of Wake Forest University; so much so, that my classroom, every year I taught, was decked out in the black and gold of the school. In addition, I obnoxiously displayed posters, pictures, pom-poms, foam fingers, basketballs, autographs, and the must-have Demon Deacon bobble-head figurine throughout the classroom. In the beginning, I did this because I was straight out of college and I needed to decorate my room with something. Without much money, I simply used what I had already collected during my college years. After a while, though, I realized that this "theme" was helping me in other ways. I want to personally thank the parents over the years, as well, for building my collection of Wake Forest paraphernalia during Christmastime, my birthday, teacher appreciation week, and the end of the year!

In North Carolina, unless you went to Wake Forest, or had a direct connection to the school, you likely do not care much for them. You are a Carolina, Duke, or State fan, as were many of my students. What ends up happening is that during basketball season (college football in North

Carolina is just a warm-up for basketball season), all my students wanted to talk about was their favorite team.

I learned quickly that was my in! I was able to have discussions about not only sports, but about college, majors, and how you get into these schools. I think some students were actually surprised that you don't just get to "pick" your college, but apply and hope that you have worked hard enough to get in.

What formed was a connection with my students, beyond the classroom and the content. They trusted me more, they enjoyed spending time with me, and they respected what I had to say (most of the time). Of course, I had fun with this, as well. There would be days when depending on the score to games between our rival teams, we would have more homework or no homework that next night. I was usually able to gain some Demon Deacon fans on those occasions.

At a Wake Forest vs. NC State basketball game with Jacob.

Knowing your students' interests and hobbies plays a big part in connecting with them. Hannah was a quiet student; one who wouldn't bother a bug and tried to fly under the radar. It was hard getting her to open up and talk with me or even her classmates. I spoke with her parents and found out she was a big *High School Musical* fan. I'll be honest, I know nothing about *High School Musical*, but I sure could learn something about it! I did a little research and got some basic facts about Troy and Sharpay, bought a *High School Musical* book for her at a bookstore, and had my breakthrough!

I began to see a new Hannah. She smiled more, participated in class, and even connected with other kids who liked the movie. While *High School Musical* was Hannah's thing, every kid is going to have a different hook. While you won't need to go out and buy a book for each student, there is value in knowing your students' hobbies and favorite things. It can be valuable in your teaching, but also in building a relationship with each student.

Connecting with your students does not have to stop at just talking about a favorite college, movie, or sport. It can be done much simpler; in fact, it can be done right as you are teaching.

In my early years of teaching, I think I did a good job looking at my students. I could usually catch them if they were goofing around or trying to do something off task. When I began working at the Ron Clark Academy, however, I learned that I was completely missing the boat on this concept of looking at my students. I learned that it is not just about looking at them to see if they are on task, but it is about connecting with them. Looking at your students in the eyes; making that personal connection that sometimes gets lost in our technology-driven world.

As I watched my co-workers teach, I could see that they were not just scanning the room, but rather deliberately connecting with each student throughout the class as they taught. And in return, the students were expected to do the same back to the teacher.

I had a personal paradigm shift when I realized what I was not doing in my classroom. As I became stronger at this skill, I noticed a huge change in not only how I connected with my students, but how much easier it was to manage behavior. When you are staring right into the eyeballs of a person, it takes some guts to misbehave right as they are staring back at you. I did not have to stop my instruction to deal with behavior issues because I could take care of it with non-verbal actions. In addition, you may have a student in your room that does not have a great home life, and the connection at school with his teacher is the only attention that he gets the entire day. Think about that. You could be the *only* person in that child's life who looks them in the eye. You could be the person who changes his life because he knows someone cares. That's powerful.

As I met teachers over time and I would talk to them about this idea of tracking, as we called it, many of the naysayers were the younger grade teachers who did not think their students could maintain that level of engagement for a sustained period of time. I admit I had my doubts, too. I have taught lessons in kindergarten, first, and second grade and I have seen dust particles that can get them off task.

So it was to my great surprise and pleasure when I got to see Ms. Cochran teach her kindergarten class. As I watched her, I could not believe the level of eye contact that these five- and six-year-olds were able to maintain. As Ms. Cochran moved about the room with deliberate intention, their little bodies turned to face her, and their eyes never lost contact with hers. It reminded me of watching cats move their heads as the flashlight moves around the walls of the room, except replace cats with kindergartners and replace flashlight with Ms. Cochran.

If some of you are thinking that she just told them to do that because I was coming into the room to observe, you have clearly never spent time in a kindergarten room. Establishing an expectation like that does not happen in five minutes. After watching her, I was curious to learn how she managed to get her students to continually track in the manner they do. I was embarrassed at the lack of depth of my question when she simply answered, "We practice."

It's really as simple as that. When you have an expectation in the classroom, whether it is tracking, raising your hand before you speak, asking permission to sharpen your pencil, it's about practicing and maintaining the procedure. Too many teachers set the expectation during the first five minutes of the year and wonder why two weeks later it has been lost.

It is so easy to tell Ms. Cochran has a special relationship with her students. Many of them came from broken homes or tough neighborhoods, so by her making those connections with her students, looking at them in their eyes and showing how much she loves them, she is giving those little boys and girls a safe and welcoming environment to come to each day.

What CAN you do? Think about your personal background. Do you have a team, interest, or an experience that the kids can connect to? Make that the theme of your classroom. Think about how you look at your students each day. Are you looking at them, trying to make sure they are on task and not poking each other with a pencil? Or are you connecting with them, taking the time throughout the day to look each one of them in the eyes and showing them that you do care about them, even without having to directly say it? Can you make it an expectation in the classroom that students track you as you move about the room, making eye contact with you as you do for them?

5.
You CAN ...
Be Lucky Sometimes

Blessed Always

There's the luck of the Irish, lucky charms, lucky rabbit feet, and lucky underwear. But sometimes, there's just plain old luck.

It's not something you plan, or something you expect, but when it happens, you just have to sit back and say, "Wow, that was pretty cool."

A few years ago, while teaching at the Ron Clark Academy, we took our fifth-grade students to New York City. We have standard sites we typically take the students to, but one of the mornings we heard that President Obama was going to be at Ground Zero doing a dedication ceremony. We had flexible plans that day, so we decided it would be neat to take the kids down to the memorial since many of them had never seen it (nor were they born yet when 9/11 happened).

We were staying in Times Square, so we took the Red Line down to Chambers St. and walked a couple blocks south toward Ground Zero. We truly had no clue what to expect, nor where the best place would be to see the memorial or the President. As we walked along the blocked off streets, we were wandering somewhat aimlessly, trying to see where the crowds were going. Honestly, it was the blind leading the blind as we asked other tourists where to go. Police officers would point us in different directions and sightseers all had their own theory on where he was going to be.

The crowds were growing larger and larger, and it was getting tougher to keep an eye on thirty kids, so we decided after forty-five minutes it would be best to head back up towards Times Square. We wanted to get back toward the Red Line, but where we were at that point, it was tough backtracking our original route, so we decided to go in a roundabout direction to get there.

As we walked north, we saw that Barclay St. was fairly empty, so we made a left turn across the street and started heading toward where we wanted to be. Before we could make it twenty feet down the road, Chandler, one of the fifth-graders, ran up to Ms. Bearden and told her that he overheard some of the policemen say he was heading down this route.

Whoa! Wait a second! There are thousands upon thousands of people crowding around Ground Zero, and the President is going to go down this street with no one on it? Ms. Bearden quizzed Chandler to make sure he heard what he thought he heard, and he affirmed he did. So Ms. Bearden said to us, "I'll be right back." She walked over to the policemen who Chandler overheard and flirtingly said to them, "I have thirty students with me who just want to see the President. One of them overheard you say he was coming down this road. Is that true?"

The officer could not officially confirm that the President would be coming down this road, but he strongly suggested that we stay here. That was all we needed to hear!

We parked our butts along Barclay St. and waited … and waited … and waited. I called my mom, who lives in New Jersey, and told her what we were doing. She was watching the event live on television, so she was giving us the play-by-play of what was happening. When I was told that Obama was about to have a private meeting with the families invited to the ceremony, all of a sudden several men in black suits and sunglasses, assumingly Secret Service, began walking up and down Barclay St. peering across the small crowd that began to form. They had people who were looking out of windows close them and asked people to back up from the street.

The kids started getting excited. They clung to the guardrail that lined the street to secure their spot. They were sure that the President was going to come down the street. My mom informed me that he was done with the ceremony and they showed him exiting the area. And then, nothing. No President, no Secret Service, no police for about three minutes. We figured he probably took another route out.

Wait a second. Out of nowhere, and I mean nowhere, a stockpile of black SUVs, sedans, and police cars come zipping down the street. Then, right in the middle, we see people flashing photos and taking video of the official Presidential vehicle as it came zooming down the street.

As it passed us, you could clearly see a person that could only be President Obama waving through the tinted glass on the passenger side of the car right at the kids. It was here and gone in a split second. But that split second felt like an eternity. The kids were screaming, crying, hugging as they all shared their (identical) accounts of seeing the President as he passed all of us.

To me, it was just one of those moments where time stopped for a bit and it took a while for everything to sink in. I don't think it was even seeing the President that made me reflect as much as it was just the amount of things that fell into line for all of that to happen. For us to give up on waiting at Ground Zero, choose Barclay Street to walk down, have Chandler overhear the officers, and then to be on the side of the street that the President would be sitting on blows my mind! Some will call this turn of events fate, destiny, or maybe even a sign. I'm simply going to call it a good bit of luck.

Later that evening, the kids and staff members on the trip talked more about the chance encounter, and it turns out that luck struck twice that day for our group. As we were taking the train down towards the World Trade Center that morning, Mr. Clark, who had stayed at the hotel in order to plan the Amazing Race that we do with the kids, had run into some detours up around Times Square trying to get to where he wanted to go. It turns out that the Presidential motorcade, along with President Obama, rode right past him, as well, as he went towards the memorial!

You do not need to bring your kids on a field trip to New York or spot President Obama to find a little bit of good luck. I remember one scorching hot August day I was eating lunch with my fifth-grade team in the cafeteria with the students. Anyone who has ever eaten lunch with me at schools knows I am a bit of a creature of habit. This began as a child when my mom would pack mine and my brother's lunch with the same bagel and ham, piece of fruit, cookies, and drink each day—for about ten years.

This routine apparently stuck with me because for the past decade I have continued my tradition of sticking with the same lunch every day at lunch. It's not a secret either. My students pick up on it and it becomes a running joke with "what Mr. Dovico is going to have for lunch that day." My lunch is not complete without toasted cinnamon raisin swirl bread with salami or ham and honey mustard, a fruit cup and plastic fork, a bag of M&M cookies, and a Dr. Pepper. There must be a Dr. Pepper. I do not drink coffee, so Dr. Pepper is my drug of choice. I drink one DP a day and it gives me my afternoon burst to finish off the day.

For whatever reason, I forgot to put a Dr. Pepper in my lunch that day. This was not good. I do not function without my Dr. Pepper at lunch. My school was a healthy school, too, so I definitely was not going to be able to find one just laying around. Then, out of a screen of smoke (not really, but that would have been cool), appeared Natalie, with a present from her family. Yes, you guessed it. She brought me in a Dr. Pepper just as a small gift that day.

You would have thought it was the Lost Catacomb of Egypt that I just saw. My eyes got big and I jumped out of my seat, raised my two arms in the air, and let out a big "YES!" I gave Natalie a big hug, and thankfully, the world was right again. Mr. Dovico had his Dr. Pepper and the afternoon teaching went as planned.

So getting a Dr. Pepper may not be as remarkable as seeing President Obama, but it's not about the magnitude of the event, it's about the impact it has on you. It's about the unexpected, the surprise, the occurrence of something that makes you say, "Wow, it's my lucky day."

What CAN you do? In your classroom, in your teaching, and even in your life, sometimes really cool things just happen. Instead of trying to explain why, or how, just enjoy it and smile. Maybe you had a little bit of luck on your side that day. When these types of events happen with your students, celebrate it, let it sink in, and remember that it is something that you have all shared together.

6.
You CAN ...
Help Others

Throughout high school, there was one club that I dedicated my time and energy towards, and that was Key Club. If you're not familiar with it, Key Club is the largest and oldest international student-led organization which provides opportunities to offer service, build character, and develop leadership. I first got into it as a freshman when some of my friends and I decided it would be a neat club to try out. The high school was renowned for its program and had one of the largest memberships in the state of New Jersey.

I participated in some community service events and did what I could to take part in the fundraisers. It was not until I transferred my junior year to another high school that I began taking it more seriously and seeing it as truly an opportunity to serve others. The Key Club at my new high school was not large, so there was more opportunity to become a leader in it. My senior year I was voted vice-president, but I took on many roles and duties beyond the title.

My crowning achievement was organizing a fundraiser for a local charity in the form of a concert. I recruited musical talent from wherever I could find them. Luckily, I had a couple of friends who were musical and some classmates who had connections to local bands. It was one of the most challenging ventures I've ever undertaken, mainly because as a student, you have limited resources and power, so I had to fight and claw to make it happen.

Now, among the "talent" were five senior guys who earlier in the school year won the Halloween costume contest by portraying themselves as The Backstreet Boys. (They were at the height of their fame at this time.) The five guys, with no shortage of confidence, but a clear lack of talent, went out there and lip-synched to "I Want it That Way" and "Everybody (Backstreet's Back)." Check out the picture below. You may recognize a certain "Backstreet Boy" in the bowing position. For fifteen minutes at my high school, we were larger than life thanks to stereotypical teenage girl reactions to guys being idiots on stage. A true highlight of my teenage years. I guess I did lose my shame long ago?

Adolescent boys trying to be much cooler than we were.

I also started a Circle K club, which is the middle school version of Key Club, my senior year at the middle school campus of our school. I wanted to find a way to open up younger students' eyes to the idea of helping others and being an active citizen in their community. It was a good leadership opportunity for me, as well, to lead middle grade students in community service projects and events. It also looked great on the college resume!

At graduation senior year, I was honored to receive the Community Service Award. As I entered college, I joined a fraternity and took part in numerous community service events once again, like Habitat for Humanity and Brian Piccolo Cancer Research (Piccolo is Wake Forest alumnus).

When I began teaching after college, I didn't know how I was going to incorporate the concept of community service into my classroom. Luckily, I didn't have to wait long to find out. At the very end of 2004 many of you may remember a massive tsunami hit Indonesia and destroyed millions of homes and killed thousands of people. This is before social media hit the mainstream, so we were getting updates from the nightly news and online reports. After winter break, my students and I discussed the ramifications of this event, and it turned into great geography and science lessons.

I began to think that this could turn into more than a classroom lesson, though. My class and I decided that we were going to raise money for the Red Cross to help the victims of the tsunami. After brainstorming ideas, we elected to create a staff and parent basketball game. We would charge admission and sell baked goods at the game to raise money. In a couple short weeks, we had a charity basketball game in January 2005 and raised over $1,300 for the Red Cross.

My students not only learned the importance of community service and charity, but leadership and real world skills, as well. I had the students running everything. From the cash register to the baked goods to "security" (Jessy and TJ were begging to do that); they had to be an active part of this event.

I also turned this into a writing opportunity. We wrote our local television station letters about what we were doing. I got a call a few days later from the station, and they said that they wanted to shoot live at the school for their morning show. They said we start at 5:00am! Guess what? We were there at 5:00am! The kids, parents, and even a few staff members, came out and shot hoops early that morning while they taped their morning show.

The following year, Hurricane Katrina hit, and it provided another opportunity to put the idea of helping others to work; we formed the Hurricane Katrina Basketball and Softball fundraiser this time. We had parents and staff members playing basketball and softball, so they got to choose what they wanted to participate in. We raised $700 this time and the kids were, once again, interviewed on television and celebrated for a job well done.

The biggest undertaking for me as a teacher, though, took place in 2008 when my running club team at Endhaven Elementary and I decided to organize a 5k charity run to help raise money for a local children's hospital. Up to that point, the team and I, made up of fourth- and fifth-grade boys, ran in 5k races around Charlotte each season to cap off our training. I'm not sure how the conversation started, but we started talking about having our own race. From there, I started calling around to get advice on how to actually make this happen.

With the help of local organizations, sponsors, and friends, the Kids4Kids5k became a reality, and over 325 school and community members helped raise $3,200 for a great organization. We shut down the streets of the neighborhood around our school for a few hours on a Saturday morning. Families came out to their driveways cheering on the participants as they ran, jogged, and walked through the south Charlotte community. I was proud of that event, and it showed what can be done when people work together and are determined to make something happen.

Volunteering and helping others has always been something ingrained in me ever since I was young. I believe that it is something everyone needs to do; it gives perspective on your own life and what you have. There is no job too small when it comes to helping others, so I always talk with my students about ways in which they can help others in their own community.

I am consistently inspired by those who find ways to "make it happen," especially when it benefits other people. I was invited to speak at a college in Richmond, VA one evening. My main contact there was a professor who helped organize the details and get the payment through. Upon arriving, however, I learned that the reason this entire event happened was as a result of a student there named Coty. Coty is the founder and president of a chapter of the Student Virginia Education Association for his college. Coty is aspiring to be a secondary English teacher, but there's more to Coty that makes him truly inspirational.

He has a physical handicap that requires him to utilize a walker to get around. For some, this might create excuses for why they cannot do something, but guess who found the money to make this event happen? Guess who found the space and arrangements for the event? Guess who the first one up and dancing was in my workshop? When I asked Coty why he put this together, he said he wanted to give people at the college and around the community a chance to have professional development and learn from the methods of the Ron Clark Academy. He told me that he looked up to us at RCA and was inspired by what we do, but in my eyes it's the other way around. People like Coty and what he is doing for others as a college student inspires me to give back even more.

Coty, one of the most inspirational people I have met.

What CAN you do? With access to social media at the touch of a screen, volunteering, helping others, and becoming socially aware has become easier and more widespread. Talk with your students about ways they can participate in volunteering opportunities in their community, but also ways in which they can be a part of larger social movements around the world. If you have a class that is interested in helping others, arrange an opportunity for everyone to volunteer somewhere, whether it is an assisted-living home, community garden or park, or a Habitat for Humanity. Every community has groups and organizations that volunteer, but it is about teaching our students *how* they can become a part of this at a young age.

7.
You CAN ...
Show Camaraderie

In life, you meet many people. Friends come, friends go, but you always remember your roots. For me, my roots are at Vienna Elementary (pronounced Vi-Anna, with a slow Southern drawl) in the little town of Pfafftown, NC (silent first f). I student taught in fifth grade at Vienna as a senior in college under the tutelage of my friend Shane, a magnificent teacher. As I was nearing graduation, I was strongly thinking about moving back to Australia, where I had spent time in college, to try to teach there or at least have some fun and avoid entering the real world.

It turned out there was a fifth-grade teacher retiring at Vienna, and I decided to apply for the position. Since they knew me and I had worked hard during my student teaching, they kindly offered me the position. I gladly took it and so began my teaching career. Australia would have to wait.

To round out my team, were five other teachers who I had begun to know during my student teaching, but little did I know at the time, would become some of the best friends and co-workers imaginable. Coming from different backgrounds and experiences, everything about us simply clicked. We laughed together, spent time outside of school together, and even vacationed together.

As a first-year teacher, it was the perfect arrangement. We showed appreciation and respect for one another, and that carried over to the students. There was no backstabbing, talking behind each other's backs, or jealously, and that is what showed the kids that they were not going to get one over on us. We were a cohesive team, and we showed the results with high achievement and having a lot of fun.

Unfortunately, as I sit down and talk with teachers around the country, professional jealously, backstabbing, and talking behind each other's back is exactly why many want to leave their building. Many teachers are a part of dysfunctional teams and it is wearing. I've learned it's not necessarily one person's fault in these situations, but sometimes personalities just don't mix. The real losers in these scenarios, though, end up being the students.

Kids are intuitive. They pick up on things, even when we as adults think we're being sneaky. If they can sense that their teachers are out to get one another, they will pick up on that and use it to their advantage. They may begin a game of "he said, she said," or even worse, try to sabotage the teacher they don't like.

If you are in a situation at your work that is tumultuous, think about why that is. Is it simply a personality difference? Has someone done something to offend the other? There could be any number of reasons, but it's always a good idea to try to work it out first. As a teacher, showing camaraderie in front of the kids goes a long way.

After teaching at Vienna, I moved down to Charlotte and taught fifth grade, once again, with a great team at Endhaven Elementary. One of my teammates, and still to this day great friend, Terrance, and I once had a bit of a tiff. There was some misinformation and misunderstanding about an award that I had won, and he was angry with me for it. I could tell he was angry with me because he was not being himself around me, but since it was the working day, we didn't have time to really talk it out. Nonetheless, Terrance remained professional and courteous while we had our children with us. When a student we both taught was misbehaving, we both dealt with him in the hallway. Luckily, we were able to figure out the situation after school one day and all was better, but I was appreciative that throughout it all we never showed any dissention in front of the kids.

One of the strongest teams I got to meet was at Allen Jay Preparatory Academy in Guilford County, North Carolina. To the principal's credit, he carefully created this team to be his start-up staff for a new public middle school, which was to start with grade five its first year. He brought together four outstanding individuals, coming from different backgrounds and bringing in different skill sets. There was the veteran teacher who brought leadership and experience to the table, the technological guru who was able to help his teammates get comfortable with the latest gadgets, the high-energy teacher who brought his smile and passion to everything he did, and the first year teacher ready to impart fresh wisdom and ideas to the team.

This magnificent team gelled immediately and ensured that they were going to create a magical experience for the students from day one. I worked with them before school started, and they were ecstatic about the possibilities that lay ahead, though had little time to put something together. By the first day of school, they were able to create a memorable first impression by welcoming the new students with music, dancing, and lots of energy. I had the chance to visit this team again during the year and was pleased to see that they have continued on their path to success by incorporating consistent procedures across the school and high expectations for each other as teachers. Most apparent with these four individuals, however, was that they were having fun together!

Showing camaraderie can be done in various ways:
1) For starters, laugh, talk, and spend time with your co-workers in front of the students. This sends a great message to the students that their teachers enjoy each other's company.
2) Treat each other like family. Give hugs, high-fives, fist bumps, or anything else that shows love for each other.

3) Look to see if you can get common clothing, like a school t-shirt that you can wear together on certain days. It sends a message of unity to students and parents.

What CAN you do? To start, show that you appreciate and respect your co-workers, especially in front of the kids. Offer compliments on their teaching, do not allow kids to talk negatively about another teacher, give them high fives or hugs in the hallway when you pass by them. Come up with common rules and expectations if you teach the same students. When students see that teachers are on the same page, even when it comes to rules in the classroom, they are more likely to think twice before trying to play teachers against one another.

My 5th grade team at Vienna Elementary School.

8.
You CAN ...
Document Your Experiences

How many of you have baby photo albums at home? Pictures on your wall? Scrapbooks from your days in school? In our personal lives, we are encouraged to keep memories of our experiences, and we often accomplish that in the form of photos or videos. With programs like Facebook and Instagram now, we can upload our lives with the touch of a button and have memories stored with ease.

As we go into our classrooms each day, there are so many great things that occur that we say, "I'll never forget that." I've said that myself, and truth be told, I've forgotten many of them. From day one, though, I made it a point to try my best to photograph, video, and write down as many things as I could. From cool lesson ideas, to projects we made, to memorable student quotes, I have albums and folders to always go back to when I need an idea or a good laugh.

This book has been created as a result of keeping many of the aforementioned items. Without the deliberate documentation of my teaching career, many of the stories you hear or photos you see would have likely been long forgotten.

As I was researching for this chapter, I could not help but stop and just laugh for a few minutes as I looked over some of the quotes I had documented. There were many that "you just had to be there for" in order to fully understand, but some are self-explanatory. To hopefully put a smile on your face, here are some of my early classics:

11/24/04
Talking to Daylon about music:
Daylon: "Have you ever heard of Meatloaf?"
Me: "Yeah, of course."
Justin (butting into the conversation): "I've had that before. It's great with ketchup."

2/4/05
After a lesson on the American Revolution and asking if any students had questions:
Jessy: "Did the colonists watch the TV to see if the British were coming?"

2/20/05
Holding five cards with numbers 1-5 on the front and questions on the back.
Me: "Pick a number 1 through 5 for your question."
Leah: "Number 3 ... that was simple. Am I done now?"

5/16/05
First grader in the hall noticing my tie (thinking it was a bowtie):
"Hey, Mr. D., nice botox!"

9/30/05
During language arts trivia questions:
Me: "Here's a hint, think of contractions."
Dezzie: "You mean like when my mama is in labor?"

11/9/05
During a lesson about abbreviations:
Me: "Is anyone in here a Jr.?"
Emily: "Well my sister is a freshman."

Obviously, anyone who has spent any amount of time with children will have their own set of memorable moments and quotes; I encourage you to write them down, look back at them often, and enjoy the innocence and sometimes ridiculousness that children can bring to our lives.

In addition to memorable quotes and moments, keep record of those great lessons you do. Teachers are known hoarders; in fact, some classrooms I have been into need to be visited by the A&E television show. I'm not saying you need to keep every lesson and worksheet you have ever done. Instead, keep an electronic file or notebook of cool ideas that you can revisit and improve upon for a new class. Avoid pulling out the same lessons year after year without learning from and adding to it from the last time. There are always things you can change and make better. That's how we grow as teachers.

If you are rather skilled at making neat assignments, lesson plans, or units, consider sharing them with co-workers or try to even earn some extra money from it! TeachersPayTeachers (TpT) is a great site that allows teachers to sell their materials to other teachers at reasonable prices. It's kind of like eBay specifically for teachers. I have used it both as a consumer and seller, and it's convenient and fun. It also doesn't hurt making a few extra bucks on items that others can use!

One of the most taken away ideas from the Ron Clark Academy after guests visit is what they have on their walls. Most schools that you walk into have bone white or pale beige walls. Covering these melancholy bricks are bulletin boards, oftentimes covered with half-hearted writing samples or a cute art project from Thanksgiving, even though it is February. When I ask teachers about their bulletin boards, I often hear that it is a mandate from administration or the district to have something up there, and it has to be aligned with the standards, which of course, must be posted under the student work.

I am not saying there is anything wrong with student work on the walls or on a bulletin board, but please make it meaningful and relevant! I am as guilty as the next for hanging up something because I had to when I first started, and I cringe at some of the pieces I once put up. When I began working at RCA, two things happened. One, I realized if I was going to put anything up on my walls, it better be "Picasso-worthy," otherwise we would get fussed at! Second, I had a paradigm shift in my thinking about what should go on our school walls beyond just student work.

Think about your home. What do you have in your house on the walls? Is it a writing sample aligned with standard 3.01? Or is it a picture of your family, with smiles from your trip to Disney World, or your children in their soccer outfits ready to play in their first game? The Ron Clark Academy was designed to make school feel like a home. In order to do that, Ron and Kim decided to put pictures of the students and staff throughout the school. Pictures of an entire class, individuals, and groups of kids cover each wall throughout the building.

Tell me you wouldn't feel good when you are walking to math class and you look over and see you and your best friend in a picture! Many of these pictures document the experience that the students and staff have at RCA. When guests are in the school, giving tours typically involves telling stories about many of the photos because they provide the history and memories of the school.

Personally, one of my best memories at RCA was captured in a picture that was hung above the grand staircase. It came from our trip to Japan when Mr. Kassa and I took a picture with our Japanese friend, Yano. Seeing that picture each time I walked up the staircase reminded me of that trip, the memories we had on it, and the blessed opportunity I had to travel to Japan with my students.

What CAN you do? Document your experiences. It'll pay dividends later on. You'll appreciate having something to look back on, and it'll come in handy when you are in need of ideas or a good laugh. Share with others, whether it is your co-worker next door or thousands of teachers around the country. Utilize technology as a means for keeping your photographs, videos, and lessons. Memory sticks are a lot less cumbersome than boxes taking up your closets! Consider putting up pictures of students, teachers, and families up on your classroom and schools walls. Seeing happy, familiar faces brightens everyone's day!

9.
You CAN ...
Teach Manners

I was recently in a local Wendy's with my son grabbing a quick bite to eat since my wife had to stay late at medical school. Quick it was not, as there was a bus of about 20 middle school kids who had beaten me to the line. I considered leaving and going somewhere else, but I hoped it would move quickly and we wouldn't be in line too long. I was wrong.

As my son and I waited in line, I had the chance to observe and listen to these preteens as they ordered their food:

"Gimme a number five with a Coke."

"Cheeseburger and fries."

"I want a Baconater with a Diet Coke."

One after another, no "please" no "thank you," not even a greeting from these kids as they approached the cash register. I was mixed between anger and disappointment that not one of these kids could use simple

41

manners as they ordered. But then, the chaperone, who was at the end of the line of kids, right in front of me, went to order.

"Yeah, gimme, a chicken wrap with a Coke. That's it."

Wow! It's no wonder the kids didn't have any manners in line. The adult, who might have been a teacher, clearly could not demonstrate them herself. As the kids sat down and ate their food, they were fairly behaved, holding quiet conversation and sitting at their tables, but I could not let go of the fact that they were absent of such simple words when they ordered.

When I eventually got to order, I was chatting with the cashier and asked her if that's how most kids order and speak to them, referencing how I thought those kids were moderately rude when ordering. She said it depends. Sometimes kids are polite; sometimes they are like this group.

So if some kids can be polite and use respectful greetings, why can't all kids? To answer this, look no further than the adults that we encounter each day. You likely see a wide range of respect and manners as you go out to eat, go shopping, or interact with adults at work. For me, I am constantly amazed by the gamut of manners that I encounter as I fly.

For two years, I was on a plane or two a week, so I have a decent sample size of people I have encountered while flying. The true tests of politeness are when flight attendants ask if you would like something to drink. How does someone respond? Is it the curt reply, "Coke"? Is it the demanding "Gimme a Coke"? Is it the polite, "Coke please"? Or is it the more genteel, "May I have a Coke please?"

Personally, I think I fall into the genteel category. Even though I grew up in New Jersey [insert New Jersey and/or rude Northerner joke as you wish], my parents raised me with manners. "Please" and "thank you" were regular vocabulary words required in our language, and this aided me some as I moved south for college, as manners are more commonplace here. Along, of course, with the expected "Yes ma'am" or "Yes sir" when responding to adults.

When I go back to New Jersey to visit my parents, I do have to be careful with the over-the-top manners because it is not as common there. I have had conversations with Southerners about how it can be seen as a bit of sarcasm if using too many polite words in one sentence. So I have learned to be aware of my surroundings when using general manners, but no matter the place, there are two common utterances that should be utilized at all times.

Please: The "magic word," as we tell toddlers when they first start talking, slowly becomes an optional expression as children get older. This should not be something that we need to remind children to say if we reinforce it as they are in their early years.

Thank you: Not surprisingly, this phrase goes right along with the first one, as it shows a sign of appreciation, something that should be shown after someone completes an act of service for you.

As educators, we do not have control over our children's home environment, so let's stop making excuses for why the kids are deficient in areas because of the home. It is what it is, so let's control what we can, and that is our classroom. When the children are in your possession during the day, whether it is for forty minutes or six hours, hold them to the highest expectations possible when it comes to manners.

At the Ron Clark Academy, if students do not say thank you after receiving something, it is immediately taken away. This goes in the case of loaning a pencil, giving out food, or offering the student an opportunity to go on a trip. It usually only takes that child losing one opportunity with something that they wanted before they learn that manners are going to be used.

Another important piece to having students maintain these expectations of using manners is ensuring that the expectations are consistent across the school. If a child goes to Mr. Howard's class for math, where they are expected to say please and thank you, but then go to Mrs. Powers' class for language arts, where it is not enforced to use these words, using manners is now seen as a chore for one class rather than a habit throughout the school.

To take the idea of manners and respect to another level, require your students to greet you as they walk into your classroom or pass by you in the hallway. One of my co-workers, Ms. Hildebrand, has established the expectation that you shake her hand and offer a greeting before you enter her classroom. The students have been trained to not enter her classroom unless this has been done.

One time, I was walking down the hall and passed by her room. Her class was a minute early and was waiting outside of her empty room. Ms. Hildebrand was making copies, so I was going to take them inside and wait with them so they could be ready. I said to the class, "Let's go in and get everything ready for Ms. Hildebrand." Immediately, I could see their eyes open wide and look at me with a sense of hesitation. I asked what was wrong and they explained that they needed to shake Ms. Hildebrand's hand first before they enter. Now that's establishing a routine!

Having manners does make a difference. I cannot tell you the number of times I have been out with my students in cities across the country and have had adults, waiters, cashiers, and complete strangers compliment the students on how respectful they are when saying "excuse me," holding a door open for someone, or saying "thank you" after receiving something.

For a couple years I was taking some of my students from the Ron Clark Academy to Winston-Salem, NC to visit Wake Forest University. I wanted them to experience what college looked like (and simultaneously brainwash them to apply to go to Wake Forest). I took Wade, Chandler, and Misaiah into Benson Hall for lunch, one of the food courts on campus. After they ate lunch, I let them get smoothies as a dessert. When the boys got to the front of the line to order, they used their manners as they are expected to. When they finished and I went to pay, the woman said to me, "These boys are unbelievable. They could teach some of the students here how to speak." She ended up giving us the smoothies on the house.

Clearly, getting the drinks for free was not the intent of being polite, but it goes to show that people are appreciative of respect and good things do happen to good people.

What CAN you do? Have discussions with your co-workers and staff about what types of language you expect to hear from your students. Pre-planning before the start of the year is a great time for this. Come up with standard language that you expect to hear from the students. Be sure that **the staff** is using this language to model it for the students. Be sure that everyone is on board: from the teachers, administration, and support staff. The students need to be expected to talk in a way that is respectful to each other and adults, and that is something we *do* have control over in our schools.

10.
You CAN ...
Eat

If you've ever spoken to a boss of any kind, and ask them how they make their employees happy, if they're being honest, many will tell you they feed them well. It's true, food makes us happy.

One of my favorite memories of working at Vienna Elementary was "Wonderful Wednesdays." The amazing PTA would provide snacks and treats in the teachers' lounge each Wednesday for the staff members. There was no better way of getting through Hump Day than being able to go grab a quick sweet during your planning period. Now, I must admit my fifth-grade team was a bit spoiled because we had our planning period first thing in the morning, so we were always privy to the largest assortment of treats before the rest of the wolverines came in and finished it off!

When I present to school staffs, I encourage the organizers to have some type of snack available for the audience. Adults tend to pay attention more after they have had something to eat. Even a small piece of candy tends to bring a smile and a burst of energy to the most lethargic of the bunch.

Any principal will tell you that their attendance at PTA meetings or parent nights is higher when they offer pizza or dinner at the events. When I was on the Home Owner's Association Board in my old neighborhood, we always had more people come to our events when we said there would be snacks there. I'm somewhat convinced that some global conflicts could be solved if food were involved. Can you imagine President Obama and Kim Jung Un of North Korea sitting down munching on trail mix and Skittles discussing nuclear proliferation? I'm calling it now!

Throughout the school year, I would do my best to bring in snacks for my kids to use as rewards or incentive. But I also found opportunities to use food as a central piece of my teaching, as well. Each year, I would do a multi-cultural unit called "Books to Bind." Early on in my career, I earned a *Teaching Tolerance* grant that allowed me to buy hundreds of multi-cultural books for my classroom in sets of six. During this unit, each student selected a book that was set in a specific country, culture, or religion. Along with numerous requirements the students were to complete during reading, we always ended the unit with a "cultural cookout."

During this cookout, each student would bring in a small dish from the culture they studied to be shared with the rest of the students. It was magnificent! Students became so vested in the book and enthralled in the culture, their dishes were extraordinary. I had students who read *The Devil's Arithmetic* (a book based on the Nazi concentration camps) bring in matzo ball soup, students who read *Sadako and the 1,000 Paper Cranes* bring in sushi and dumplings, and students who read *The Circuit* bring in tortillas and beans.

In all, there were over fifteen different cultures represented and that led to a great diversity of food that students were offered. Interestingly, many students had eaten some of the food that was brought in, but had no idea that it was associated with that particular culture or the history of it. The kids were required to have knowledge of the foods they presented because before they could go wild with sampling the food, I invited parents to join in on the Cultural Cookout and become the learners. Parents were asked to go around to the different student stations and not only sample the foods, but ask the students questions about their book, their projects, and the culture in which they studied.

It gave a great opportunity for the students to become stronger presenters, and it held them accountable for their research and learning. They enjoyed being able to share their hard work and took pride in the fact that they were "experts" about a book and a culture. The parents were impressed at the level of learning that had taken place and were proud to see their child taking ownership of their education.

If you are going to do something like this, one discussion that you have to have with your students before the Cultural Cookout day is what a sampling means. I learned this the hard way. The first year I did the cookout, the parents had finished doing their part, so I let the kids begin their sampling of the food. Big mistake!

Most of their plates looked like they were at a China Buffet restaurant; food stacked a mile and a half off the plate, falling on the ground and making a mess in the multi-purpose room. I was infuriated and about had an aneurism, but I was also embarrassed because I had not taught the students my expectations of what to do during the food sampling.

The next year, I had an entire mini-lesson on how to sample food. It went much smoother and my blood pressure decreased dramatically. I did the "Books to Bind" unit for many years across several different schools I taught at. As I transitioned to teach at a Title 1 school, where parent resources were not as abundant, I looked to the community to assist and managed to get several restaurants around the town to donate food to the cookout—for FREE! While I made improvements to the unit as it developed over the years, the culmination with the Cultural Cookout always remained and it stood the test of time that when you feed people, they will come.

What CAN you do? Depending on what subject and grade level you teach, how can food be incorporated into your content? In math, can you use cakes to teach fractions? In science, can you use baking to teach chemical compounds or physical changes? My "Books to Bind" unit truly combined language arts and social studies, as it allowed the students to read their novels while studying a particular culture. The food brought together a research component that forced students to read and learn about how that food is relevant to the culture.

An amazing assortment of food for the Cultural Cookout.

11.
You CAN ...
Press Reply

I have always made it a point to respond to emails within 24 hours of receiving them. There are two reasons for this:

1) It's polite. In the business world, as I'm told, it is expected that emails are responded to within 24-48 hours. Is that not reasonable in the education world? Yes, I know there are those who are saying I have students all day, meetings before and after school, families to take care of, and on and on. The point is, make it a point to do it. If you make it a deliberate task to check your email and respond to them, it becomes habit, just like brushing your teeth and showering (I hope).

2) I'm a little OCD. I have this horrible obsession with not allowing more than fifteen emails in my inbox at any given time. The only way to maintain that is to respond to what's in my inbox and then sort them into folders. I cannot stand looking at my inbox and seeing that there are two pages of emails. My friend Gina is laughing right now because we go back and forth on this. She will have at

any given time 1,500 – 2,000 emails in her inbox. When she wants me to break out in hives, she shows me her inbox just to mess with me. She says she can just search for the email she needs when she needs it. I like everything neatly sorted and arranged into appropriate folders.

The ironic part of my habit of responding to emails quickly is that it surprises parents. Parents continually thank me for responding to an email quickly like it is something unique. So often I hear teachers complain that parents are angry at them for their child failing or getting into trouble. What this typically boils down to is a lack of communication. If an issue arises in class, let the parent know. This will also help avoid the parent say, "If you had let me known about this earlier, I could have taken care of it."

The key is communication. Yes, it takes time to write emails and respond to parents, administration, and other staff, but it is necessary. Just like grading papers, making lesson plans, and going to meetings, we need to communicate to maintain the professionalism that we always want as teachers.

If you come across an email that is going to take a while to respond, and you do not have the time at the moment, simply write a temporary response explaining that "This issue is important and I want to make sure I give it due diligence. I am short on time at the moment, but I promise I will respond to you in depth as soon as I can." This shows that you care about the concern or the issue at hand and you are not ignoring it. The person will appreciate the acknowledgement and now you have bought yourself time in a respectful and professional manner.

When you receive a "nasty gram," as we used to call them from a parent, an email explanation may not be the best means of communication. In this response, you may want to consider saying, "I appreciate your concerns and I think this is an issue we need to discuss face to face. Would you be open to meeting with me tomorrow morning before/after school?" By sending this response, you are showing that the concern is valid and that you are interested in addressing it. Holding a face-to-face meeting with an angry parent will usually turn out better than an email anyway. Most people are not as crass face-to-face, and by buying yourself an evening or two between this email and the meeting, many parents will cool down if they were upset with something. Firing back an email to their initial one with emotions attached will likely cause the issue to unnecessarily intensify.

My brother Marc, who is an educator and high school soccer coach, once had a classic parent nasty gram from a father who was outraged that his daughter wasn't receiving more playing time as a senior. There were several mitigating circumstances surrounding why this girl was not playing more, but this father had his horse blinders on and there was going to be hell to pay for my brother not playing her.

Now, my brother is fairly thick skinned and stubborn, so his first reaction was to simply ignore this electronic berating. When he told me about it and what he was going to do, I strongly encouraged him to write a reply with the advice I previously stated above. I told Marc to write that "he understands his frustrations and he would be happy to meet with him, and the athletic director, to discuss this since it was a complex situation that would be best talked about in person." The last thing you want here is an email war!

Marc took my advice and sent the email as I suggested, copying his athletic director. The parent shot back another email rehashing his previously shared sentiments and stating that he wasn't going to meet with him. Although this parent was still outraged, Marc put the ball in this parent's court, and the invitation was open to meet with him. The fact that the father chose not to only hurts his case in the eyes of the administration. Marc's athletic director and principal had his back the entire time because he copied them on each of his communications, clearly showing that he was opening up the door for further discussions outside of email war. Marc's decision to communicate with this parent in a timely and professional manner saved him from the embarrassment of having to explain all of this later on to his bosses.

The majority of emails that you receive are going to come from co-workers. Emails from co-workers deserve the same attention and respect as one coming from a parent or administrator. If the co-worker has reached out to you to ask a question, make a request, or offer something, provide the response or feedback they are in need of in a timely manner. At times, they may actually be waiting on your response in order to proceed with something, so be aware of the situation. If you are short for time and it is a response that can wait, simply write back, "Hey, I'm swamped at the moment, but I'll get back to you as soon as possible." The nice thing about co-workers is that you do not need to be as formal in your writing, and they will often understand if something needs to wait, but they appreciate your response as much as anyone else.

It is vital to maintain records of your communication throughout the year, especially with parents. At the end of the year, on more than one occasion, I have been asked by my principal to show evidence of communication about academic achievement about a child when they might fail a grade. It is reassuring to the principal when I can provide dozens of communications with the parent from throughout the year talking about either concerns or strategies being employed for their child. Even quick emails with an update on something they did well, or a good grade from a test, means a lot to the parent and shows the administration you are being pro-active in your communication.

On one memorable occasion, I was sitting with my administration and fellow teachers discussing a student whose parent was outraged that no one was reaching out to her about her child failing. The child was lazy and simply did not do the work. He had the ability, but just chose not to complete assignments or study for tests. As my co-workers and I began looking through our records, we found that we had not only emails, but text messages and face-to-face documentation that we had informed her of his progress. In the end, we had over thirty documented communications from various teachers all informing her of the same thing. She was quiet after that.

As our schools become more diverse, it is imperative that we communicate effectively with *all* parents, despite any language barriers that may exist. Many parents in our schools do not speak English, and so it is important that we find ways to still communicate with these families so that they, too, may feel a part of their child's school experience. I have been in several schools where for any electronic or print communication piece that goes out, the principal ensures that it is translated into other languages spoken by the school's parents. Many principals use staff members, students, or community members to assist with this. The important thing is that parents are receiving the necessary information in order for their child to be successful.

One of my former fifth-grade students, Samantha (though she typically went by Sam), spoke fluent English and Japanese. About a month into the school year a family with a kindergartner entered our school from Japan, and they spoke zero English! My principal called up to my room and explained that she needed Sam because this family was struggling with filling out the paperwork and getting their questions answered. Sam beautifully assisted this family, and she became a fifth-grade helper for this little kindergartner who was trying to learn English. Each time either the principal or the classroom teacher needed to communicate with this little girl's family, Sam was more than willing to assist. If the little girl needed some help with something or was having a bad day, Sam was like a big sister to her.

Being aware of the resources within your own school and in your community to increase communication can strengthen the bond between the school and home for many families that speak different languages.

What CAN you do? Be a communicator. Even if you do not like using email—pick up the phone, write a note, hold a meeting—do whatever it takes to communicate with your students' parents. Document everything! If you have paper notes or signed copies of tests, make a folder for the child so that you can pull it out when needed to prove that you have been pro-active in your communication. Be smart about the content of your email. If you are not sure how an email is going to be perceived by the reader, have another adult read it first and provide feedback. That should be an indicator as to whether or not you should press send.

12.
You CAN ...
Be a Storyteller

In the spring of 2011, I was blessed to have the opportunity to travel to South Africa with the seventh and eighth graders at my school. Having a love for travel, South Africa had always been on my bucket list. It has such rich history, from the studies in early man to the colonization of the British to Nelson Mandela and the Soweto uprisings; you can literally follow human history as you travel through the country.

As a part of our trip, we had the opportunity to visit a beautiful cultural village called Lesedi, situated in the Magaliesberg mountain range. In the village, you can find an authentic showcase of the traditional culture of some of the well-known African tribes, who find their home in South Africa. As you walk about the village, each tribe has designed a traditional portrayal of their culture, and they invite you to experience what life would be like for them.

Amongst the tribes you will hear music, see clothes making, and experience life inside their huts. There are customs and rules you learn along the way demonstrating how each tribe lived and survived. We decided to split up as a group and I was one of the teachers with the seventh graders.

I was up in the front of the line with Nissaba, one of my girls. You need to know that Nissaba is one of those students who will try anything. If there is something dangerous, new, or just plain odd, Nissaba is usually game for it.

So the class and I approach the Xhosa tribe, one of the villages that you visit. As you walk upon the village walls, there is an arch that you walk beneath to enter. As we were about to enter, a woman dressed in traditional Xhosa garb pops out from behind the wall and greets us.

She says, "Welcome to the Xhosa Village. Before you enter, it is customary that you sample one of our traditional snacks." It was getting close to lunchtime, so I was excited for a little food in my stomach.

That feeling didn't last long. The woman proceeds to pull from a table a woven basket full of what looked like little brown turds. Yes, I said it. Little brown turds. Dried up little brown turds for that matter. Picture something about the size of a peanut, with varying shades of turd brown, sitting in front of you and this woman says that we need to eat one. My stomach went from famished to on the verge of vomiting.

I had to think for a moment how I was going to get out of this. There was no way I was going to eat this thing in the basket. Well, before I could figure out a way out of it, Nissaba pops one of those suckers in her mouth like it was an M&M. My only thought at that point was, "Shoot," here one of my students goes and eats one of those things and now I'll never live it down if I don't do it, too.

Our motto at the Ron Clark Academy is "No Fear," so if there was ever a time to embrace this, here it was. So I finally took one of these things and held it in my hand. It felt kind of like a small piece of beef jerky, with a rough texture and somewhat hard exterior from being dried out and cooked. I held my nose and counted to three.

At three, with all of the seventh graders behind me watching, I popped it into my mouth. I took the first chomp and it crunched. Whatever I just bit down on definitely had some exterior that was hard and dry because I could feel pieces of it sticking to my teeth, like a piece of popcorn getting stuck in your mouth. Almost teasingly, I could also taste a hint of salt that coated it. Immediately after, however, another texture surfaced. No longer was it just the crunch, but now a swampy sensation began. It was sort of like Gushers candy, where you bite through the candy coated surface, but then it's a flavored jelly underneath. What I would have done for a flavored jelly at this point.

There was flavor alright with what I tasted, but it was definitely not strawberry or grape. The gush was more like a nasty juice, one that had sat out in the sun too long and had become rotten. At this point, I was committed to finishing what I had started, so I continued chewing this horrific snack. Chomp after chomp I polished off this offering until it was no more. It took several seconds, which felt like hours, but finally the task was complete.

I managed to ask the woman what I just dined on. She informed me that I had just munched on what is called a mopane worm, a delicacy in many parts of Africa. The crunchy part I tasted was, in fact, the outer part of the mopane, which had been cooked and salted because, yes, the salt certainly made it that much more appetizing. Next, the succulent juices I endured were the intestines of this creature.

Upon doing research when I got home, I found out that the mopane worm is actually not a worm at all, but rather a species of moth called *Gonimbrasia belina*, more specifically a large edible caterpillar, and is an important source of protein for millions of Southern Africans. You learn something new every day!

What I hope just happened over the last ninety or so seconds is that you went through emotions—possibly ranging from disgust to laughter, but probably more disgust. I hope that you read that story with ease and with excitement. For me as a teacher, that is a hook. If you have ever worked with kids, they love anything disgusting, weird, or out of the ordinary.

By starting a class off with that story, I now have the kids in my grasp. I have them interested in what is to come next. Honestly, I may go about my teaching in a fairly normal manner for the rest of class, but telling that story got them interested, and that's a victory for me.

As I travel around to observe classrooms, I rarely see teachers using personal stories or engaging tales to hook the students. It's one of the easiest and most practical (it's free) ways to engage your students. You do not need to buy fancy resources or create extravagant handouts to get the students interested. Becoming a good storyteller is something anyone can do with the right mindset and practice.

Now what if you don't have a cool story like eating a mopane worm or something wild and crazy?

MAKE IT UP! Come up with something! The kids will never know! If your life is not that exciting or you cannot think of something really neat that you did, just pretend that you did. I have told the most absurd stories about opening up bakeries, being a 1970's disco dancer (FYI I was born in the 80's), and getting trampled on by a kangaroo in Australia and breaking my collar bone (I did break my collar bone, just not in that cool of a fashion, but I can still show them my scar). The kids bought in to each one of these stories, and as a result, I was able to get their full attention for my lesson right after the story.

After offering your story, then you can make the connections to your content. If I were to use my mopane worm story, what could I be teaching about? Perhaps culture, insects, customs, or geography? Throughout my lesson, I could continue to reference my original story in order to draw the connection back to the element that got them interested in the first place.

By the way, Nissaba, my student who ate the worm first, had another awesome experience after eating the worm. As we entered another village, there were women with a bucket rubbing a muddy substance onto the ground. The women explained that a part of their job in the village is to make a firm floor for their hut out of mud ... and cow manure. Lovely.

As the women asked for any volunteers to try out rubbing the mud/manure mixture into the ground, yup, you guessed it, Nissaba jumped at the opportunity.

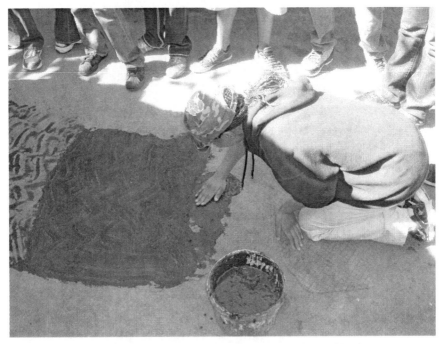

Nissaba rubbing mud and manure into the ground.

What CAN you do? Think about your experiences in life, from the funny to the absurd. Don't worry about finding a story that fits perfectly into what you are teaching if you can't think of one. A good story can be molded so it fits into many paths. Enhance the story by adding extra details and animate yourself when you tell it so the kids truly buy in. After you have the kids hooked, weave the story throughout the lesson so the kids can continually be brought back to what engaged them. Aim to pull at different emotions, as well; the greater the rollercoaster that the audience goes through, the more likely you will draw them in.

13.
You CAN ...
Incentivize

I debated whether or not to put this chapter in the book because I'm a bit embarrassed to say that I did this. I think there are ways to engage and excite students without promising something at the end. But in this single situation, I had no choice. This was a big deal and I was left with a big decision to make.

It was the end of the year Field Day competition. At many schools, Field Day is a fun, relaxing chance to bring the parents in and watch the kids run around a bit. Mr. Dovico and Mr. O'Neal missed that memo. Shane O'Neal was my mentor and is a wonderful friend of mine, but we are also both as competitive as they come. There were five fifth-grade classes, but Shane and I were clearly the most into it.

A couple of days before Field Day, classes are supposed to assign students into the races and competitions that go on throughout the day. There are some fun ones, like the free throw and hula-hoop competitions, but then there are some serious ones, like the mile run and the wheelbarrow race. Then there is the four by one hundred meter relay—my favorite. Four students race back and forth with a baton trying to be the first team to finish. For years, I dominated that race. I'll be honest—I stacked my team with my fastest kids to all but guarantee victory.

This year I decided to empower the kids more and let them self-select the events they wanted to be in. By fifth grade, the kids knew their strengths and typically sorted themselves into appropriate races and events. Enter Damian.

Damian is the student that I had to remind to catch up with the class as we walked down the hall. Damian is the student who when we got in line, he was still putting away his books. Physical movement was not his strong suit. Yet for some unbeknownst reason, he decided that he was going to enter himself in my four by one hundred relay team. Oh boy.

Flash forward to Field Day and it's time for the four by one hundred relay race. I have three other students aside from Damian who were extremely fast. My best bet was to let them go first and build up such a lead that it would be nearly impossible to lose. We were ready for the race. Where's Damian? Seriously, the kid signs up for the race and is not even there for it. Then there he was, on the side eating snacks. I broadcasted, "What are you doing?" He replies, "I'm hungry." *Really?!*

You're about to run a race and you're eating snacks on the side. I took a deep breath and thought. There has got to be something to motivate this kid to run fast. I need him to have something to run for. Air Heads! Yes, Air Heads! Throughout the entire year, this class, for some reason, was hooked on Air Heads candy. I bought them in bulk as prizes for various trivia games or rewards, and Damian was infamous for conniving his way into getting Air Heads from classmates at any opportunity.

I said, "Damian, how would you like to earn *five* Air Heads?" It was like a dog perking up when hearing the door open. "I need you to go out there and run faster and harder then you've ever moved in your entire life. If we win this race, you sir, have earned yourself five Air Heads of your choice. Got it?" Sold.

That boy went out and ran those hundred meters like they were the last hundred meters he'd ever run. People who knew him for years just stood in bewilderment, as the boy who typically made it difficult on himself going from door to desk, just beat several other able-bodied competitors in a running race. Holy cow! The apocalypse was upon us and pigs just flew, but most importantly, Dovico's Deacs won the race!

If I seem a little over the top and a bit carried away with Field Day, I am. I am an athlete and competitor and I like the joy of winning. But more importantly, when I show the passion and excitement toward these events, it carries over to the kids. They get more motivated and focused. Or at least that is what I am telling myself.

Many schools I have visited have used simple, yet effective means for incentivizing the students. More than once I have seen a classroom or school economy where students are earning "money" in order to buy items or earn rewards. Some more advanced programs even include checking accounts and banking procedures so the students are learning real life skills, all the while working towards something that they want.

My second grade teacher, Mrs. Parisi, is my first memory of a reward system during my schooling. We earned "Parisi Pennies" in her class and could purchase items like candy, notebooks, pencils, or the big homework pass! To this day, I can still recall how exciting it was to earn those pennies and then be able to buy something. In one particular instance, we had special guests that were coming in, and we had some students in the class who could have easily ruined it given the chance. Mrs. Parisi told us that if we were behaved during the visitor's time in our room, we would earn ten pennies each! Talk about hitting the jackpot! That was big time! Needless to say, we were complete angels that day!

What CAN you do? I am not promoting or encouraging incentives all day, every day, but sometimes incentives in certain situations can work wonders, especially when you are creative with them. Kids can do amazing (or previously believed impossible) things when given the right motivation. If you have a dire situation for performance excellence, and you need to truly convince students to push themselves like never before, think about what can motivate them.

14.
You CAN ...
Suit Up

If your first thought upon reading the title of this chapter was Barney Stinson, you rock! If you have no idea what I'm talking about, no worries, I'll explain.

Barney Stinson, played by Neil Patrick Harris (aka Doogie Howser, M.D.), played a womanizing, cocky, yet comedic businessman on the television show *How I Met Your Mother*. When it comes to clothing, though, there is no choice but to "suit up," meaning put on your best because you dress for success.

As educators, we struggle to find our place in society as professionals. We kick and scream against critics to be considered professionals and experts in our field, but there's a responsibility that comes along with that. I am continually blown away by the lack of regard for how some educators dress when entering the workplace.

On numerous occasions, I have come face to face with teachers who are coming in to teach with sweatpants, hoodies, inappropriately logoed t-shirts, and sneakers that look like they double for yard work. I admit, I have done my share of casual Friday jeans and school-pride t-shirt, but casual does not have to mean sloppy or unprofessional.

Understandably, there will be a wide range of interpretations for what is acceptable for teachers to wear, but administrators need to take an active role in addressing this touchy issue in order to make clear expectations for staff members. Personally, I have worked at schools that cover both ends of the clothing spectrum. At one school, jeans and a polo shirt were the norm, while at another school I had to wear a suit each day. I can't say I was a better teacher in one atmosphere or the other, but I do believe I was treated differently in the two scenarios.

When I was dressed more casually, the kids were more lax and parents acted similarly. Parents would use my first name to address me and have more joking conversation. In comparison, when I was in a suit, both kids and parents treated me differently. They spoke more formally and addressed me as Mr. Dovico. It simply felt more formal. In return, I felt more like a professional. I would even argue that I walked around with a bit more swagger when I had my suit on.

I have experienced before my very eyes that the way we dress does play a role in how we are treated.

When I was in college, I would order a Subway sandwich for dinner at least a few times a week. For three years, I would order a BMT (add bacon), no cheese, with honey mustard, and oregano. Yes, there is my creature of habit coming out again. Each evening, I would go up and do my best to make small talk with the Subway servers. They responded with the typical "Hi" or "Thanks," but it was hardly conversational. Fall of my senior year is when I student taught, and I wore dress pants and a button down shirt each day, with a tie on Tuesday (I'll explain why in a minute). Like some magical spell, I transformed into a new person at Subway. The servers treated me differently. Now it was "Yes, sir" or "How are you today?" as I walked up to the counter. I was blown away. These are the same people who for three years treated me like just another student, but the second I put on my professional wear, I was treated differently.

After my student teaching, I returned to my plebian status as another college student, but I always remembered how I was treated during that student teaching time frame. It made me think about how I look, especially in front of my students and their parents, and I have taken pride in looking professional as I go into work each day.

I actually have looked forward to being able to find fancy dress shirts and ties. Stores like Kohls and Target are always having great deals on dress clothes, so I do not have to spend more on those clothes than I would on any other clothes I would be wearing to work.

Before we end this chapter, I need to explain the importance of wearing the tie on Tuesdays. My mentor teacher during student teaching, Shane O'Neal, always wore a tie on Tuesdays, and only that day. It took me a few weeks to realize that it was always on the same day. So I asked him one week what was up with the tie on Tuesdays. He explained that Mondays can be tough because it's the first day back from the weekend, but there's an inherent excitement to see the kids again, so that gets him through the day. Wednesdays are hump day and getting through Wednesday meant that you made it through half of the week. Thursdays were so close to the weekend that the excitement begins building up for your weekend plans. And then, of course, Friday speaks for itself.

And then there's Tuesday. What's there to get excited about on Tuesday? It's the stepchild of the days of the week. Shane said that waking up on Tuesdays was always a struggle, so he needed to find some way to make sure he felt his best when he walked into the classroom. He decided that looking good would help him feel good. So each Tuesday he wore a tie, and sometimes a jacket, as well, into school and that would help energize him to get through the day. I liked that he saw that by dressing up he was giving himself more confidence and energy, and I remembered that as I student taught with him and entered into my own teaching career.

One great outcome of tie Tuesday was that over the course of the year, many of the students picked up on this, and not before long, some of the students would wear ties on Tuesdays, as well. It was a neat tradition in the room and one that can certainly be replicated by others out there.

65

What CAN you do? Reflect on the clothing you wear to school each day. If you are struggling with classroom management or parents at all, can it be that you are not presenting yourself professionally enough? Especially as a young teacher, it is important to differentiate yourself from your students, and your apparel can be an easy and effective way to accomplish that.

15.
You CAN ...
Be Humbled

I was that guy. The guy who came into my first year of teaching convinced I was going to solve the world's issues, conquer every educational road-block, and be the teacher that everyone loved. Cocky? Perhaps. Confident? Without a doubt.

Either way, I was excited to start my school year. I had a foolproof way to celebrate my students each week. I called it the "Deac of the Week" and it was voted upon by the students in the class. For the first several months of school, it went flawlessly. The students voted and I would post the picture of the Deac of the Week on my website and bulletin board each Monday. The child would also receive a candy bar and was applauded.

As the year wore on, it became obvious that the same students were being voted upon as student of the week. There were about four or five students who had received the award at least three times each. Most of the other students had received it once, but the same students kept receiving it. I look back now and realize it was quite a popularity contest, and as a result, it was ostracizing some students. I began making sure those students who had not yet received the award "won" it, even if it meant me doing some discretionary decision making, though I hadn't gotten to the entire class yet.

It was March and I had an IEP meeting with a student's parent and the special education teacher before school started. The meeting went fine and I finished in time to make it to start the school day. The special education teacher had left the conference room, and I was cleaning up my materials getting ready to head to my classroom. The parent then gave me the words that you never want to hear: "I'm not done with you."

Oh oh. It definitely did not have a "I want to give you a present" kind of tone. I said to her, "Yes?" with a smile and curiosity. Inside I was scared to death. I was by myself in this small conference room with no direct route to the door and a visibly frustrated parent. For the next minute (which seemed like an hour), the mom fussed at me because her daughter had not won Deac of the Week yet, and each week she spent the evenings upset because the same "popular" kids were winning it. I was ruining her confidence and desire to go to school.

Man, I couldn't have felt smaller. I tried to explain that this was simply an incentive program so that students who truly wanted to earn the recognition could step up in their academics and behavior. The students would recognize this and she would be voted as the winner that week. It was the best I could come up with in that tense moment, and looking back now, it was a copout answer.

I am all for earning recognitions and awards, but the structure of this program was flawed. Its design lent itself to a popularity contest, and instead of just admitting that, I tried to come up with an excuse for that parent by defending it. She was clearly upset and not satisfied with my answer, but I explained that I needed to get to class, and we could continue the conversation later if she liked.

The old saying, "waking up on the wrong side of the bed," would have been a welcomed way to start the day compared to how this day had started. I had no confidence as I began teaching that day; all I could think about was that meeting. At the end of the day, I had to have a serious sit-down with myself to figure out what I could do to fix this.

I realized quickly that I had been served a big piece of humble pie by that parent. The first thing I decided to do was write an email to the parent to say that I was sorry that her daughter was feeling this way, and the intention of the program was never to make any student feel that way. I also added that I would consider a new format for the award so that it was a more equitable process.

Would you believe that the week after this meeting the student whose mother had just ripped me apart won the Deac of the Week? I didn't fix it and didn't say anything to the rest of the students. What I did notice was that the student was working harder and had changed her attitude toward others. She was being more cooperative and friendlier. Perhaps her mom had motivated her? Maybe it was just a coincidence? Whatever the reason, the students noticed it and elected her Deac of the Week.

I emailed the parent and I made sure I emphasized the fact that she earned this on her own. After that, the student continued to work hard for me, and the mother actually ended up being a great room mom for the rest of the year. She even helped chaperone a special trip I organized for the class.

Looking back, that day in the conference room sticks out in my mind. I was brought down to earth by this mother, and frankly, I needed it. I had been overly confident in my decisions and thought that anything I did was clearly the right decision. As a first-year teacher, I did not have all the answers. I sure thought I did, but I was clouded by an overinflated perception of my abilities and decision making.

As I meet first-year teachers now, I see many who remind me of myself. They are confident as they tell me about their discipline systems and incentive programs. They, too, believe that their actions will change the world within the first six months of their career. There is a fire in them that I do not want to extinguish, but I also want them to learn from my mistakes. I share with them my story and tell them that there will eventually be a humbling experience that they will have. It is an induction ceremony into teaching. A rite of passage, if you will. That does not mean that they need to lose that fire when they have this moment. I never did. What I did *outcome*

do was learn to think more about repercussions and evaluate decisions better.

In subsequent years, I eliminated Deac of the Week and instead shifted to more deliberate celebrations for students at any moment. I focused on giving students moments to shine based on accomplishments inside or outside the classroom, including academic achievement, leadership, behavior, sports, and performing arts. This proved to be much more effective since I could highlight students for a variety of reasons and let the class know about great things their classmates were doing each week.

What CAN you do? Be humble. If not, someone is bound to do it for you. It can be uncomfortable and upsetting when this happens, but if it does occur, learn from it. Think about your decisions and how they affect your students. Frequently look to garner feedback from your students about your teaching and programs that you have in your classroom. This is how we grow as teachers and individuals.

Admit failures
Regroup
Class mtg

16.
You CAN ...
Utilize Your Resources

At the moment, I am flying from Atlanta to St. Louis. We have been going through turbulence for about fifteen minutes now and my stomach is not enjoying it. I am, however, sitting next to a gentleman I was talking to for a few minutes before the plane took off, and it inspired me to take out my laptop and type while the plane goes through what feels like a midair rollercoaster.

I learned that the gentleman is a veteran Delta Air Lines pilot, and he was connecting to another flight he had to captain. He began explaining to me why we were bumping around in the air and what he has to do as the captain to navigate these rough spots. As someone who has never flown a plane, it made sense the way he was explaining it, and it was interesting understanding something that I had always just accepted as a pain in the neck as I fly.

As he asked what I did, I explained that I was an educator. I added that it was people like him that we need in our classrooms. The simple yet detailed manner in which he was able to explain turbulence to me is something that the kids could also benefit from. When I taught units on weather or force and motion, this is someone who would have been wonderful to have explain why these things matter. The kids are always asking, "Why does this matter?" Well, here's someone who can explain why it matters and how it is important for his job.

I believe it is important to have guest speakers come in to talk about their area of expertise. They add value, engagement, and relevance to what I am teaching. They also supplement my teaching with facts and knowledge that I would never have known. Over the years, I have "recruited" a number of people to come to my classroom to help me further the students' understanding of our subject matter.

In college, I had a minor in social studies, so I took a number of history, sociology, and government classes. My favorite class, by far and away, was a class called The Civil War and Reconstruction taught by Dean of Students, Paul Escott. He is a world-renowned expert on the Civil War and has written a number of books on the topic.

On the first day of class, he managed to memorize all thirty plus students' names and still begin teaching content all within the hour. He moved at a fast pace, but one that was engaging, interesting, and humorous. His tales of the battles and facts concerning the strategies of the two sides was impressive and it remains one of my favorite courses I have ever taken.

As a first-year fifth-grade teacher, I felt quite prepared to teach the Civil War, as we covered a full timeline of United States history. We used to joke that we taught from Native Americans to "Brangelina." In our social studies books, there were the typical facts and information that you would expect to see about the Civil War (or the "War of Northern Aggression," as I learned was the proper terminology when living in the South). They talked about the first shots fired at Fort Sumter and the bloodiest battles at Antietam, but it just didn't compare to what I had learned from Dean Escott.

I decided to send Dean Escott an email and explain that I had taken his course a couple years before and would love it if he could come to my school to talk to the fifth graders about interesting facts on the war. He happily agreed. To be honest, I didn't know what to expect since this is a college professor who was about to talk to ten-year-olds. The information he taught us in college likely would not have worked with the kids. When he came in to give his lesson, all my worries went away because he told about all the stuff that kids love: blood, weapons, battles, and heroes. It was perfect!

Another memorable guest was my friend Dr. John Cull. John was my roommate at this time and a first-year medical student. I had to teach a lesson on the brain and how it functions, and I found myself struggling to give more than the basic parts of the brain and what they do. I asked John if he would be interested in coming in and talking about what he was learning as a medical student. He did one better! Instead of just talking about the brain, he found a way to bring one in!

Dr. Cull showing a real life brain to the kids!

As he removed the brain from the formaldehyde, there was a mixed feeling from the room. As you can see from the picture, Jacob was a bit squeamish, as were some of the other kids, but others were excited that in front of them stood an actual brain. Personally, I thought it was really neat. John proceeded to point out the various cortexes of the brain and all of their functions, but he also showed how injuring certain parts of the brain can cause various disabilities. The important part for me is that it brought relevance to the topic and having the brain there was a great engager.

I would love to say that I am an expert in everything I teach, but I certainly cannot. My knowledge and resources only go so far when it comes to content, so I find it beneficial to call upon experts to support my teaching and enrich the experience for my students. There are experts in almost any field you teach in and around your community, so I encourage teachers, as I conduct training, to think about what human resources they have available to them.

To do this, I typically have school staffs make resource books. First, I give each person a few index cards and ask them to think of people they have personal connections with, such as family, friends, or neighbors. Then I ask them to write down on the index card the person's name, their profession, and then their own name so that co-workers know who the contact person is. Then I give the cards to either a curriculum coordinator at the school, or the principal, to make a file box. Within the box, I usually recommend breaking the cards into subjects, like business, media, science, athletics, and so on. From there, teachers can access the box to find people who have connections to individuals or groups that can supplement what you are teaching in the classroom.

Another idea is to get to know what your students' parents do. While some of them who work may not be able to volunteer on a consistent basis, if they have an interesting job, they may be able to help your class in other ways that will educate the kids.

yep! Great ideas

Krispy Kreme donuts make any lesson just a little bit better.

Ally's father was the manager of a Krispy Kreme donuts store in Winston-Salem. If you've never had this delicious circle of greatness, you are missing out. When I first started college, I had never had Krispy Kreme before since they were mainly found in the South at that time. When I discovered them, I feel safe saying that I became addicted, legitimately addicted. If they had a group rehab, I could have used it. I averaged one or two of the donuts *at each meal* every day. That's about three or four donuts a day, times seven days a week, times the four months I went on this binge, and we're looking at around a couple thousand donuts my first semester of college. My arteries truly loved me. I should have invested stock in Krispy Kreme, looking back!

Somehow I survived this binge, but luckily the habit tapered off as the years wore on. When I met Ally's dad, he said that he would be happy to teach the kids about the business, and he also mentioned that he could bring in samples. Sold!

He came in with some of his co-workers and talked to the kids about how to operate a business and the process of making the donuts. He kept them in line by promising a free sample at the end if they were behaved. Those kids had never been so focused in their lives!

Like any responsible teacher, though, I was first in line to make sure that the donuts were safe to eat!

What CAN you do? Schools are typically the centerpiece of a community, so businesses and individuals are often willing and eager to help in any way they can. Think about units or lessons that you teach throughout the year and consider ways in which you can have a person or group come in to either add additional knowledge or relevancy to the topic. Call, email, or write letters to people you wish to bring into the classroom and explain that you would appreciate their time in helping educate the children on their field of expertise. How could anyone say no to that?!

yes
good point

- Government
  field Trip
- Rafting
get them to come
  & teach a
  Business lesson
- YGP
- CCOE

17.
You CAN ...
Visit Your Students' Homes

In my early years of teaching, I was at fairly middle-class, suburban schools. Many students came to school with a good educational background and decent behavior. After a while, I wanted to make a change and go to an inner-city school. I was fortunate enough that my former principal was now leading a Title 1 school, and she was looking to bring in some new teachers. I took advantage of the opportunity and joined the school the next year.

I immediately saw the differences. It wasn't so much what was going on in the classroom, but more so what I was learning about what the kids experienced outside of school. So many of them talked about what was going on in their neighborhoods or in their own home, and it was disheartening. From crimes to drugs, weapons to fights, these young students were living life like I never personally experienced growing up.

I had a few particularly challenging students that year, and I wanted to learn more about where they were coming from, so I arranged visits to their homes. Kirk was my first priority. He couldn't stand school! He wanted out in the worst way. I wanted to see why. I arranged a meeting with his mom at his house and brought along with me the school resource officer for extra support.

We drove to a part of the city that I honestly did not know existed and drove up into the half dirt, half rock road with about five tiny houses on it. I had the address and went up to ring the bell. No one was home, so we peeked in around the window and saw the lights were out. It was frustrating because we had confirmed the meeting just that morning.

All of a sudden, we saw a few people peer out from the door across the road and one shouted out, "You from the school?" We said yes and we then saw Kirk with his mom and some other people we did not know. Kirk and his mom walked across the graveled street and unlocked the door to their house. When we walked in, we were immediately met with a cloud of smoke and a stained smell to the air.

The first thing I noticed was a hoarder's collection of candy boxes sitting on a table next to the sofa. We're talking dozens of boxes of candy, some of which were still wrapped up in the plastic. I later found out that she is known as the "candy mom" on the street and kids go up and give her a dollar for a piece of candy. It's her primary income.

I asked Kirk to give us a minute with his mom so we could talk. I explained to his mom that when Kirk was on, he was a joy to have in class. He contributed with thoughtful answers and was fun to be around. It was unpredictable when those moments would be, though. Sometimes he would fall asleep upon walking into class. He would threaten to fight anyone who looked at him funny. But much of the time he just basically wanted to leave.

I asked her to explain to me what Kirk does when he gets home from school. She said he usually goes and hangs out with friends for a couple of hours when he gets home, then comes home and plays video games with his siblings, has something to eat, and then goes to bed. The way she was explaining this made my teacher eyebrow raise just a bit. She was tentative in her answer and seemed to be coming up with things as she talked.

I asked her what friends he was hanging out with—she didn't know. I asked her what kind of games was he playing—she didn't know. I asked to see his bedroom—all I saw was a mattress in a barren room. I obviously knew something was peculiar here, so I didn't want to press the issue more. I spoke to Kirk for a couple of minutes, but did not want to pry much with his mother there.

The next day, I pulled him aside and discussed things that were on my mind. I eventually found out that he was hanging out with 14- and 15-year-olds from the neighborhood (he was 10). They smoked and drank, though he promised me he was not doing it. He wasn't playing video games because the game system was broken. The barren room was, in fact, his bedroom. He shared that bedroom and that mattress with his two younger siblings. No wonder he wasn't getting any sleep! He said that he was always complaining about hating school because he was simply tired.

That was the worst of my home visits, but it stuck in my mind. I was not going to make excuses for him in my class, but I knew he needed help, as well. I pushed to have him be a priority with the family services department at our school, and I did what I could to give him class materials and one-on-one help with his assignments so he could do them in my presence. Unfortunately, he was suspended several times that year for fights and bringing a weapon to school. But after I went to his house, I believe he saw me in a different light. He respected me for showing that I cared.

Home visits can also be a lot of fun. At the Ron Clark Academy, we made it a point to visit each one of our incoming students' homes. I have gone to dozens of my students' homes, and it is a great information piece for me to know where they are going home to each day. Oftentimes, parents will also cook up a little snack or meal for the visit, which I admit is kind of nice.

One year, Mr. Clark, Ms. Bearden, Mr. Bruner, and I went to Mark's house for a visit. When we went in, they had a legitimate feast prepared for us. We are talking several courses, salads, meats, potatoes, greens, breads, and desserts. Wow! That was impressive! We ended up staying there for quite a while and enjoying the family and getting to know them better. Unfortunately, that was the first house on the list that afternoon and we still had about a dozen to go that day! And, of course, each house had something for us to eat.

I had forgotten about what it was like to have your teacher come to your house until I saw the faces of my students when we walked in. It can be nerve-wrecking and exciting at the same time for kids. When I was younger, my mom owned an embroidery business that was set up as an addition to the back of our house. It was actually funny at times because some of her customers would drive to our house in their work vehicles. In one day, we would have a police car, fire truck, and hearse all in our driveway. Luckily, our neighbors knew what was up because that could have led to a whole bunch of neighborhood gossip!

Several of my teachers were customers of my mom for many years, so it was always exciting when I knew they were coming over. My brother and I were good students, so luckily, my mom typically didn't have to worry about parent-teacher conferences during those visits, but it certainly kept us in check knowing that my teachers would be coming to my house and could easily talk to my mom, if they wanted to, about us.

By visiting your students' homes, you are sending a message to the student and the family. You care about this child and you are going to do what it takes to be there for them. The effort to come out to the house alone has made a statement, and from there you can truly build a great relationship with the families.

What CAN you do? There are Kirks in schools across the nation. Many of you have taught someone like Kirk and have stories similar to what I experienced. It is not easy holding a student who hates school to a high academic and behavioral standard while still being compassionate. Understanding where they are coming from is a powerful tool. Knowing their circumstance will help you reach that child in smarter ways. By going to their home, you can be on the lookout for things that they are interested in and items they may need. You will also be building a base for the relationship that can be of great value during the school year. Use all of this knowledge to help find ways for the child to succeed in your class.

Realistic?

18.
You CAN ...
Be Clean and Organized

This chapter will be dedicated to my mother. A woman who vacuums her vacuum, does not use the grill or stove because "it's for show," and used to clean after our cleaning lady left. It was not easy growing up in the Dovico household. My brother and I were brainwashed at an early age that if it was not clean, it was not livable. The sound of the vacuum and the smell of Windex are some of my earliest childhood memories.

My mom also had rules. Oh, there were many rules. First, there are never to be shoes in the house—ever! If your socks were dirty, especially after playing outside, they were to come off in the laundry room, which sat right inside the garage door. From there, we would be required to tiptoe up the stairs and straight into the shower. Next, the kitchen table had to be washed first with the wet sponge to get up the crumbs, then sprayed with 409, and finally wiped down again with another sponge. It was time to wake up in the morning when the vacuum came into our bedroom. If food ever left the kitchen, medieval torture devices were perfectly permissible for punishments.

Everything also had its place. My mom had an uncanny ability to detect when anything was moved, even slightly. It wasn't pretty when she saw something was moved from its rightful spot. Of course, that was the opening my good friend Jay needed back in high school. Jay is a natural prankster. He loves to make people laugh and he wanted to have some fun at my mom's expense. In our kitchen there were miniature ketchup and mustard bottles I brought back for her from my trip to Spain. They were on a shelf in the corner. Jay decided he would switch the two bottles one night when we were hanging out in the kitchen. The next day there was no "Good morning," it was only my mom shouting out "Why are my ketchup and mustard bottles switched?" Busted.

It was a strict environment for sure, but it was all I ever knew. Well, until I went to friends' houses and saw how the other side lives.

This upbringing instilled many values and habits that I still carry with me today, though to a lesser degree than my mother demanded. I discovered how embedded my learned behaviors were when I started teaching. It drove me nuts when things were left on the floor or there were messes anywhere in the room. I would stay at school an extra twenty or thirty minutes some nights just to get the room clean and organized to the point where I would not have to think about it when I got home. Maybe I was brainwashed more than I thought?

The summer after my first year of teaching, I won a trip to Japan as a Japan Fulbright Memorial recipient. I traveled with one hundred other educators from around the country to Tokyo, and then to a homestay in Nikko with a lovely family. Honestly, I think Japan was created for my mom. That is the cleanest country I have ever been to. Even in Tokyo, a city with millions of people and no trash cans on the street, you would be hard pressed to find even a gum wrapper on a sidewalk.

When I went to visit schools in Nikko, I observed a cleaning system they had where at a designated time every student in the school stopped and cleaned the building from head to toe. It was the most impressive human machine I had ever watched. Kids were sweeping floors, cleaning bathrooms, wiping down desks, and so on. I thought that was a great idea, and it inspired me for the next school year.

That summer, I went out and bought brooms, mops, sprays, sponges, and any other cleaning supply that OSHA would probably yell at me for. I created a job wheel in my room, where each week the students rotated into a new job and completed their task for the five minutes we did our "classroom cleanup" as I called it.

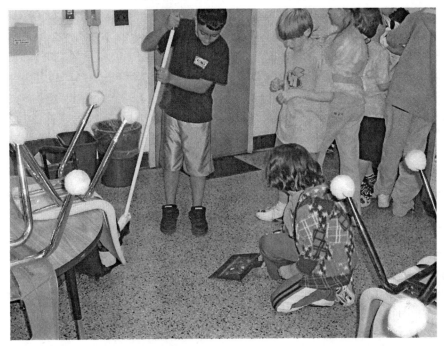

Students taking part in "classroom cleanup."

Quickly, I discovered we had a problem. These kids had no clue how to clean. The sweepers would start in the middle and sweep to the wall, the desk wipers would clean before the desk sprayers sprayed, and the window cleaners about broke the windows trying to wipe them down. What a mess! Like a lesson on fractions or punctuation, I had a cleaning mini-lesson. I modeled how to properly clean each part of the room in an efficient and effective manner.

I did my classroom cleanup for several years, and the janitors always appreciated the extra help when they got to my room. Some parents, over the years, also appreciated the kids being given lessons on how to clean. Though some would jokingly mention that they clean more at school then they do at home.

My cleaning and organization tendencies traveled with me to the schools I taught in. It was never long before my students and co-workers discovered my habits. When I arrived at the Ron Clark Academy, I offered to take on what they called *osoji,* which was similar to what I was doing in my classroom for all those years. I also gained the reputation of being a bit obsessed with my vacuum. Unlike my previous schools, my classroom at RCA had carpet. Well, if there is one major difference between flooring and carpet, it is that carpet shows everything. From dirt to crumbs to little pieces of paper, everything shows up on carpet.

So to start the day, between classes, after school, and any other time I could find, I would vacuum my room. I admit, it was a bit obsessive, but it bugged the daylights out of me seeing things on the floor, so I did it. I would also frequently recruit members of my "clean team" to come in and help me wipe down the desks and chairs just to get rid of those germs.

In addition to being clean, one must be organized. My desks had to be touching each other perfectly, my paper stacks were precise, and my room had to be in correct order before I left for the day. It's no wonder I would not get out of there until 7:00 most nights. There is nothing better, though, than walking into your room the next morning and it looks perfect.

I tried to convey this message to my co-workers, particularly the co-founder of RCA, Kim Bearden. Kim is a good friend and a wonderful human being, but her room made me break out in hives. Her materials and papers were always everywhere, and I would secretly sneak into her room some-times just to straighten things up. Whenever I was in her room, she would apologize for the way it looked because she knew it drove me nuts. I kept telling her to join me on the dark side. She would be happy to be less stressed.

Well, one summer she decided to take the plunge and organize her entire room into bins and files. It was a transformation like no other. She was so happy she took a picture of her closet and put it on Facebook. I felt like a proud parent.

Her room remains a success story to this day. She has joined the dark side and maintains a neat and orderly classroom. She is now looking to spread her cleanliness to others in need by starting up a help group. (I made that last line up, but she is certainly qualified to if she wants.)

What CAN you do? Everyone has different thresholds of clean and organized. For instance, mine is nowhere as strict as my mom's, but it is much more than my wife's. As a teacher, you can teach your students to be organized with their materials and clean when it comes to hygiene and germs. It is more powerful when you are modeling these behaviors, so ask yourself if you are practicing what you are preaching. If your classroom is beginning to look like an episode of *Hoarders*, please call me (or my mom) for help.

Asking for Storage bins for Christmas :)

"Yes

I clean up at the end of each day.

Responsibility

19.
You CAN ...
Share Ideas

During a trip to South Carolina to conduct professional development, I met a teacher who was interested in working at the Ron Clark Academy. I had seen her teach and she was strong. She told me a bit about herself and her background, and there were quite a number of attractive qualities that would make her a strong candidate. I talked to her a bit about what it was like there and said that one of the most important parts is being able to share best practices and strategies while educators visit the school.

Her face scrunched up like I had just told a really confusing joke or something. I asked her if she was curious about something. She said that she does not share her resources. They were created for her students and she didn't want other teachers stealing her ideas.

Needless to say, she was not a candidate after that. Nonetheless, this brings up a broader point in our profession. Unlike insider trading and espionage, there is no need for teachers to keep their best ideas hidden away like the Lost City.

Let's be honest, we're not in it for the money, so no teacher is making more money than the next by hoarding away top-secret ideas. In fact, you're really shooting yourself in the foot in the eyes of an administrator when you are not willing to help make others around you better by sharing ideas. Principals need strong instructional leaders who can help others around them!

Be willing to share in your own school. Be a teacher leader. Ask your administrator if he or she is willing to give you five minutes to show a strategy that you have used in your classroom that has worked well. Invite co-workers into your classroom to watch you teach. *no not safe*

As I work with administrators and provide feedback after spending time in their schools, one of the most frequent items of advice I offer is to establish a peer-to-peer observation program. These are deliberate, planned observations where a teacher will observe a co-worker for approximately 20 minutes. They then reverse the roles later that day or sometime that week. Afterwards, the two teachers sit down to debrief, ideally with an administrator or academic coach present.

This type of practice serves many purposes:

1) It allows teachers to see what another is doing. Rarely do teachers step outside of their four walls to watch each other, and this is providing a time to promote peer learning and pick up new ideas.

2) It leads to valuable discussions. The idea of the debriefing period at the end is to discuss what each other saw. It is important to be open and honest in these meetings. Teachers should never take anything personally, but rather as opportunities to grow as educators.

3) It holds teachers accountable. When these observations and discussions are taking place on a frequent basis, it is expected that teachers are making changes and adopting new ideas that others can observe.

4) Hearing feedback and suggestions feels differently from peers than it does a boss. You tend to listen with a different ear when your equal is offering it.

like positive feedback ☺

I have personally enjoyed the opportunities I have had to observe my co-workers. It's allowed me to see how another teacher handles the learning or behavior issues that I experience in my class with the same children. I have acquired strategies that I did not think of and also offered ideas to the teacher based on my perspective.

Dr. Jones is a phenomenal math teacher at the Ron Clark Academy. She loves math, like really loves math. As in, she has math equation stockings that she wears with her dresses. That's a love for your content! At one point during the year, she and I decided to do peer-observations with the seventh graders. She would come into my room when I taught them, and I would go into her room when she taught them. That class was getting a bit spring-feverish, so we wanted to pick up a few tricks from each other to deal with them better. I noticed that Dr. Jones had certain people sitting next to each other who worked quite well together. I noted that and made the same change in my room. I also made observations that I was able to share with her, like cutting down on transition times and giving out consequences quicker.

For those administrators or bosses reading this, encourage your teachers to share best practices. Create the platform to promote teacher leadership and evoke valuable conversation. Allow time at a faculty meeting to have teachers present, utilize teacher workdays to collaboratively share lesson ideas, or implement a peer-to-peer system as described above.

Another way to share ideas that does not require people to have to sit down and talk (since time is precious at school) is to have an idea board posted in your teacher workroom. I observed this at an elementary school in Louisiana. The principal had a gigantic board that teachers were asked to share what they were doing in the classroom that others might be interested in. For example, one of the ideas that I saw posted was a second-grade teacher who said that she was playing a math game with playing cards that required the students to add cards up quickly in order to build the largest pile. If another teacher was interested in learning more about it, they knew they could talk to her. By sharing ideas and resources, we are making each other stronger and building the school community tighter.

Another great idea is from my friend Joyce Estrada. As a Spanish teacher, she wanted to find a way to support and enhance the content that the students' other teachers were doing. Joyce had a board up in her room and students were asked to occasionally put sticky notes up that stated what they were learning about in their math, language arts, science, and social studies classes. By doing this, Joyce was able to find ways to incorporate content from other classes into her Spanish class. For example, if the students were learning about body systems in science class, she could teach body parts in Spanish and support what they were learning in science class all at the same time. The great thing about it is that she did not have to find the time to sit down with the science teacher in order to find out what he was teaching.

What CAN you do? Don't be a hoarder! Share your best ideas with co-workers and the larger teaching community. There are many websites and places you can share ideas, and there are always teachers looking for help from others with successful strategies. If you are a veteran teacher, look to guide or provide support for struggling teachers with ways to engage the students or plan effective lessons.

20.
You CAN ...
Start a Club

The award winning LEGO robotics team.

I know the story. Teachers have grading, lesson plans, emails, meetings, paperwork, families, and much more on their plate. Oh yeah, there's that thing called teaching, too, on top of that. I get it, it's a lot. I'm not refuting it.

But … there's always a but … who are we there for first and foremost? I hope you said the kids. When situations allow, there is nothing more rewarding than creating and growing a club or organization at your school.

It takes initiative to organize a club. It requires time that you could be doing other things. It commands dedication and commitment from students and adults. There are hoops to jump through and preparation that is at times challenging.

I speak from experience. Over the years, I have created and co-created clubs like a Model United Nations team, LEGO Robotics team, video makers club, running club, and a track and field team. It was downright challenging sometimes to get these things off the ground, but I always kept my goal in mind. I wanted to provide opportunities for the students to cultivate a love for something that could stay with them beyond their years with me. In some cases, it gave students a chance to be excellent at something, building confidence and leadership.

Corey was a firecracker of a kid. Never short on energy, he was a likable young man from teacher standards. Stayed out of trouble, was friendly, and had a good sense of humor. The problem was that academically he was weak—really weak. By fifth grade, his mom had been told time after time how "Corey's a great kid, but he is struggling in school."

After you hear that for enough years, no matter how good of a kid you are, it wears on your confidence. Corey was nearing that stage. He simply seemed depressed coming to school, especially as the work got even more difficult.

When I created the running club, he was one of the first to sign up. His dad (who was extremely athletic) told me how it was all he could talk about for weeks leading up to the first practice. All of the energy that Corey always had sure came to use on the team. He was a natural. We ran for miles and miles and he never got tired.

Other students started noticing how good he was at running and were giving him a lot of praise. Soon word got around how talented Corey was in this club, and teachers began praising him, too. Over time, I began seeing a little more pep in his step during the school day. I would love to say that there was a fairy tale ending here, and he became an honor roll student, but that did not happen. He did somewhat improve his grades because I did not allow anyone on the team who was failing a class, but he had to work hard for a C.

I can only imagine how good Corey must have felt having his classmates and teachers praising him. I am not sure what Corey is up to these days, but I am confident that he is now a student-athlete who impresses his teachers and coaches.

I want to share a funny story stemming from my time with Corey on the running club. Each winter we ran a 5k race to end the season. It was held downtown, and afterwards, we had a cookout at my condo. When we started the race, Corey and I said that we were going to run together. He wanted to use me as his pace man. When we were about halfway in, I could see that Corey was inching ahead of me but did not want to get too far ahead because we said we were going to run together. I told him he's welcome to go and speed ahead. I did not see him again until the finish line!

The most rewarding club I have started was the Model United Nations (UN) team. If you are not familiar with it, the Model UN process simulates the real United Nations, which is the largest governing body of countries worldwide. Ambassadors come together to discuss pressing issues like hunger, the environment, nuclear weapons, etc. Model UN allows students in middle school, high school, and college to discuss, debate, and come up with their own resolutions on the issues presented to them.

My team at the Ron Clark Academy, along with my co-founder Gina Coss, was widely successful, and we found it to be one of the most enjoyable experiences with our students. We would attend conferences around the world and meet students from countries that we had only learned about on the map. It challenged my students to think harder, become stronger speakers, and most importantly, learn tolerance and acceptance of others.

Ms. Bivins, a seventh-grade teacher at a school in Stone Mountain, Georgia, and I were talking about Model United Nations during one of my visits to her school. She seemed intrigued by it and well-studied on world issues as we talked about topics that are discussed. I casually mentioned she should start a team, and without hesitation, she replied, "I'm on it." Her "I got this" attitude was so refreshing and encouraging. In an age when people find excuses to avoid doing anything more than the minimum, it was exciting for me to see her eagerness about starting this team. Having started a Model UN team from ground zero, I shared my experiences and ideas with Ms. Bivins. Within two weeks, she had a team, permission slips, practices scheduled, and financials ready to participate in their first conference. She wasn't kidding when she said she was on it!

I've learned there's not a magic formula for starting clubs or teams other than straight up hard work and dedication. Many times, "figuring it out as I go," has been my best strategy because, otherwise, I don't think I would have ever started these clubs had I waited for every answer. I have sought resources and people with experience to guide me in my early days of starting a team, and in turn, I have tried to pay it forward by assisting those who are now in my shoes.

What CAN you do? What are your interests? Do you have a hobby, a sport, or a skill that you can share with your students in an after-school club or activity? If it's something you enjoy, your passion and excitement will roll over into what you do, and it will not seem like something you are being forced to do. By offering these opportunities to students, you may be giving a chance to a student to feel success and accomplishment.

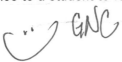

21.
You CAN ...
Be a Cheerleader

As a teacher, I often find myself playing the role of a father figure, big brother, doctor, psychologist, handyman, counselor, maid, cook, social worker, technician, and several other things that I am not sure if I am qualified for. By far and away, though, the most frequent role I find myself in is that of a cheerleader. No, I am not doing front handsprings and stunts—more on that later, though. I can barely touch my toes, but I can be a voice behind the encouragement and support many of my students need to achieve.

When parents, co-workers, or teachers I observe and work with ask me what they can do to help their child, my first response is typically cheer them on. You don't need to know algebra, Shakespeare, or the periodic table in order to be a supportive person. Much like a cheerleader encouraging the team, a simple "You got this" or "I believe in you" is sometimes the thing that a child needs to hear in order to try.

Right out of college I lived with a couple of good friends in a three-bedroom apartment on the second floor of a pretty nice apartment complex (at least compared to the standards of college living). Below us was a family who had a son in sixth grade. I had met the dad a few times just in passing and, at some point, I mentioned I was a teacher. One day the dad asked me if I could tutor his son.

I asked him questions about what the concerns were. The dad said that his son was getting into trouble at school and he was not doing his homework. He was a hot-tempered kid and did not like people telling him what to do. Clearly, he was doing a great job of selling me on this gig!

I reluctantly agreed and started out by just meeting the boy. I went down to their apartment to meet him and the rest of the family. Holy cow! I just stepped into a reality show or some practical joke because this was nuts. First, there was a bird flying around the house. Yes, a bird. Then, there was the apartment in general. It was the same layout as ours since it was just below us, and it looked like it had just gone through a battle or a tornado. Things were just flung everywhere. Finally, there were the parents. They cussed and screamed in general conversation. Who knows what it sounded like when they actually got mad. Nothing about this was looking good.

Meeting the son, I found out that the reason he did not do his homework was because he decided his video games were more important. His parents didn't care or check to see if he had done the assignment, and as I found out later, they told him he was too dumb to do it anyway.

When I started working with him (in my apartment, not the bird sanctuary), the first thing I made sure happened was the video games went away until homework was finished. After that, I tried to rewire his thinking about his abilities. I pumped him up by giving him fun technology-based assignments since he liked working on the computer. I used positive words around him, but remained strict with the expectations I laid out for him.

We had a good system going for a while. He worked for me and studied the things I needed him to study. His grades picked up and his parents were thankful for the tutoring. It reaffirmed for me that positive interactions and encouraging words could make a difference.

Unfortunately, there is not much of a happy ending here. The boy did not show up for a couple of weeks for our tutoring. I went downstairs to knock on the door to see if everything was ok, and when the dad answered, he was acting quite suspect. I asked if we were going to continue the tutoring, and he said we were going to put it on hold for a while. What I eventually found out, through the teaching grapevines, was that the boy tried setting his school on fire (unsuccessfully) and was facing pretty serious charges. The family eventually relocated and I never heard from them again.

While hearing of that news was clearly disappointing, I knew that I had done my best to give this kid an opportunity to hear something positive. Even years later, I remember this kid and it reminds me how important it is to give our students words of encouragement in class, because you never know if they are receiving it at home.

I will end this chapter on a high note, though, with one of my more embarrassing stories. Back in college, a couple of my fraternity brothers were on the Wake Forest cheerleading team. One of the guys was in my pledge class and he was always hanging out with the female cheerleaders. I thought, "Well, that's a good way to meet good-looking girls." So during my sophomore year I asked my friend about the cheerleading team, and he said to come out to a practice. There weren't too many guys willing to be on the cheerleading team, so they were always excited when a new guy came out.

At my first practice they tried teaching me how to do simple chair lifts. There is nothing simple about a chair lift when you do not go to the gym and are not particularly strong. I'll be honest, it was a bit embarrassing because these girls are barely 100 pounds, and most of the guys in there are lifting these girls with one hand! I managed to get through the practice, but I could not lift my arms for the next three days. I was clearly not fit to be a cheerleader. It turned out that I was not going to be eligible anyway for the team since I was going abroad in the spring to Australia and you had to be on the team for the entire year—whew! Got out of that one.

What CAN you do? While being a male cheerleader in college was just not meant to be, I could bring the positive attitude and spirit that a cheerleader offers to my classroom. As a teacher, your encouraging words and support can make the difference in a child's life. A simple "You can do it" each day shows that child that you do believe in them.

22.
You CAN ...
Have Your Students Help You Propose

Ladies: If you have a boyfriend who you are hoping pops the question soon, DO NOT read this chapter. Instead, give him this book and tell him to read. We men need to stick together and you will thank me later. I promise.

Fellas: You're welcome.

I have an amazing wife. She is low maintenance, lets me keep a man cave in the basement, and detests shopping. She could not care less about material things, which has helped over the years in the financial department under a teacher salary.

When we first started talking about the marriage thing years ago, she always told me that she didn't care about anything to do with the process except the proposal. It had to be special. She reserved the right to call a "redo," if necessary. I agreed to the terms and began thinking of something spectacular when I decided it was the time.

I dug deep into the creative files and realized that I have the best ammunition a guy could ask for—kids! Jaclyn has always been fond of my students, and she got to know each of my classes just as much as they got to know her. It was a no-brainer when I decided to include them in my mastermind scheme.

The Plan: It was going to be my final year at Vienna Elementary due to my relocation to Charlotte the next year to join Jaclyn there. At our fifth-grade commencement ceremony we always had a speaker say a few inspirational words to the class. I asked my colleagues if it would be ok if Jaclyn spoke at graduation and told about her personal journey and the challenging times she faced in middle school. They overwhelmingly agreed. That's when I told them the real reason I wanted her there! My idea was that at the end of the ceremony, we were going to give Jaclyn a few "gifts" as a thank you for being the speaker. I would be the last one to give a gift, and that is when I would go down on one knee and do the deed. You would have thought I just told my co-workers that *they* were going to get proposed to! They were so excited.

The Preparation: A couple of weeks before the commencement ceremony, I had my high school student intern help me make giant signs that said, "WILL YOU MARRY ME?" on individual poster board pieces. I then carefully explained to my class that they were going to take part in the biggest scheme of their short lives. I first swore them to secrecy (actually, first I had to tell them what a scheme was—vocabulary is so important); with the punishment for a blabbermouth being the repetition of fifth grade (they probably did not realize I didn't have that kind of power). From there, we ran through what this would look like on stage. I had fifteen students take one card each and practice lining up in the exact order in which the question was spelled. This was not a time for typos! We practiced the drill like it was an inbounds play for a basketball team. No water break until it was perfected!

<u>The Execution</u>: It was the day of the ceremony, and I'll admit, I was a bit nervous. I don't get nervous for many things, but this was definitely one of them. Jaclyn made a wonderful speech and the ceremony went well. I was called back up onto the stage by my assistant principal and began calling up a couple of students to give thank you gifts like flowers and a card. Then I called the entire class up on stage. The students passed out the giant cards and Jaclyn began to get distracted. I explained that I loved her and wanted to spend the rest of my life with her. I don't think she was paying attention, to be honest. I had the students turn their cards around (praying they were in the right order) and got down on one knee. That got her attention. Bam! Operation proposal was a success!

It turned out one of the student's dad was taping the ceremony and managed to get a copy of the tape for me. The proposal is now forever enshrined on YouTube and can be seen if you type in "Adam and Jaclyn's Proposal."

The proposal.

What CAN you do? Fellas, if you are a teacher, and are looking for some creative way to win major points with the girlfriend/fiancé/wife, utilize the best resource you have available—your students! Have them write poems, make cards, create a song, or anything else that will make everyone else go "Awwww." If you are not a teacher, find someone who is and plead with them to help you create that magical moment or gift for the anniversary present that you forgot about until the day of (yes, I'm speaking from experience).

Gentleman: Good luck and, if necessary, you can now return this book to the original reader and pretend like nothing happened.

23.

You CAN ...

Tell About the Good Ol' Days

One of my favorite books to teach is *The Watson's Go to Birmingham – 1965* by Christopher Paul Curtis. It's not only a well-written novel, but it highlights racial and societal relations during a trying time in our country. These topics lead to excellent discussions about growing up in a different time and what it must have been like to be discriminated against because of the color of your skin.

As I was teaching the book, though, I realized that many to most of the students were having trouble understanding not so much the discussions on race and family, but how people lived without cell phones and laptop computers. In *The Watson's*, there are references to record players, radiators, and Betty Boop (yes, they all laugh at that one). It's hard for them to fathom a household without a 60" flat-screen plasma television with Netflix and DVR.

Now I was still but a thought in the 1960's, but I have taken time over the years to listen to people who did live during the "good ol' days," and I wanted my students to be educated about society that preceded them. There is so much to learn from the past, and I believe whole-heartedly in that old saying, "Those who cannot remember the past are condemned to repeat it."

There is cultural and educational value in teaching our students about those who came before us. I don't just mean giving facts about wars and history, but talking about how people lived, how our lives have evolved, and even how future generations will look back at us. Have you ever thought about how society will look in thirty, fifty, or even a hundred years?

I have ... and here's my prediction ...

In fifty years (I'll be in my 80s; hopefully, still alive and kicking) we will continue to find ways to utilize technology to make our lives even easier and enjoyable. I believe the use of 3-D technology will evolve into holographic technology in every household, where televisions will no longer be just on a screen, but rather projected into holograms with depth and realism. I am envisioning an explosion of electric cars to take over mainstream society. No longer will we need gas stations, but rather recharge stations along highways, where cars can recharge their batteries in a matter of minutes. Finally, I believe that chartered outer space travel will become affordable and routine for average citizens. Space stations will provide unique opportunities to explore and experience a world that was once distant to us.

I know that many of these things already exist, but until they are mainstreamed into society, they remain somewhat of a pipedream for the average person. I do not claim to be Nostradamus, but those are my predictions. For the record, I have never been good at selecting NCAA basketball tournament brackets or fantasy football teams, so take these predictions with a grain of salt.

To bring it back to my original point, find ways in your classroom to talk about how life was before our students' time. During my *Watson's* teaching, I always brought in people who could discuss what life was like during the Civil Rights era from a personal perspective. One of my favorite individuals to come in to talk to the students was an African-American woman named Dr. Woodard, who taught during this time period in an all-black school in the city.

She, like many of the previous speakers I had brought in, said that she never really thought about everything being segregated at that time because "that's just how it was." She only knew of things being separate, so she never gave it much thought that her life might have been different from a white teacher's. It wasn't until people began marches and violence broke out in her neighborhood did she realize that there were people trying to make changes. She said that she did not join in the marches since she wanted to continue to teach in the classroom, but many of her friends and family members were arrested for protesting and marching.

My most memorable guest speaker came during a unit on the Holocaust and the Jewish experience during World War II. Through a student's mother, I managed to get in communication with a sharp and engaging woman named Suly Chenkin. Ms. Chenkin was born in Lithuania in 1940, right at the outset of the Nazi invasion of eastern Europe. Being Jewish, the family feared for the worst, and prepared appropriately for the inevitable raiding of their town. In 1944, Suly was given a "sleeping potion," as she called it, put into a potato sack and onto a cart, and then thrown off at an appropriate time so that she could be whisked away by a family who would take care of her during this time in what is now Israel (then Palestine).

Both of her parents and her grandmother were taken by the Nazis. Her grandmother, deemed too weak to contribute to the movement, was sent to the gas chambers. Both of her parents survived several death marches and any number of randomly selected assassinations. They both grew weak, but hung on through it all. Amidst harrowing conditions and unbelievable bravery, the family was eventually reunited in 1947 in Cuba.

Out of the 40,000 Jewish citizens of the Kovno Ghetto in Lithuania where she was born, only five percent (2,000) survived. Of those people, three were Suly and her parents. Ms. Chenkin shared that it was simply a miracle that not only she and her parents survived, but that somehow they were able to be reunited.

This brief summary of Suly Chenkin's life in no way gives justice to the emotions presented as she retells her story. It is hard to keep one hundred fifth graders absolutely silent for thirty minutes, enthralled in your words.

Her story managed to do it with ease, and it was one of the most engrossing experiences I have ever experienced.

Unfortunately, people as sharp as Ms. Chenkin, who experienced this piece of history and are willing to talk about it, are far and few. With each year that passes, we lose individuals who can educate us on the past like this. Fortunately, I did videotape her speech and was able to share it with subsequent classes so that they, too, may hear history from the first-hand account of this miraculous woman.

With technology at our fingertips these days, it is quite easy to find videos, interviews, music, and educational programming that teaches about the past. Sites like YouTube, TeacherTube, TED Talks, History.com, BrainPop, and so many more, provide wonderful educational tools for teachers to enhance their lessons.

One of my friends, Susan Barnes, a magnificent language arts teacher, is a master at teaching history through various forms of media. One of my favorite units that she teaches is on the Harlem Renaissance. While teaching about the African-American cultural movement that blossomed during this time, she draws from music and videos on the greats like Duke Ellington and Fats Waller, and shows evidence of how jazz and the blues broke color barriers and became a part of mainstream America. By using a wide range of media resources, she is allowing her students to experience history beyond just reading about it in a text.

What CAN you do? Never assume. Over the years, I have had to teach what 8-tracks, sock hops, and beehive hairdos are as we came across them in our stories and texts. It provides a great opportunity to talk about what life used to be like before our students' time. If you are not old enough to have lived through some of these things (like me), try to find people who did to come and talk about it to your students. Hearing about history from someone who lived it inevitably brings in a certain passion as they speak. It is that passion that will engage the students and give them a reason to care.

24.
You CAN ...
Tip Your Humpty

I'm the first to admit, those kindergartners scare me. They're just so ... little. I swear I am going to accidently step on them or knock them down as I dash from place to place. I'm also as sarcastic as they come. My jokes go right over their heads, and it drives me nuts.

With all that being said, there are teachers made for those munchkins, and they are good at what they do. One of my favorites to watch is Cindy Resendes. Ms. Resendes actually started off teaching in fifth grade and moved out of there as quickly as if I had started out teaching kindergarten. She is an outstanding teacher and is absolutely made to teach the wee ones.

Her academic and behavioral expectations are through the roof. She is able to have her students working at high levels within the first weeks they are in her class. But she knows how to have fun, too. She is a former dancer and includes movement and song into pretty much everything she does. Her annual Cinderella spin-off play is a huge hit at her school each year. Her bubbly personality makes her a perfect fit for the young ones, and most importantly, she loves what she does.

She calls her students the "Lucky Stars," and they are all about show-ing what it looks like to be the best. I observed her teach a math lesson on measurement one day where, within thirty minutes, she integrated sci-ence, reading, and writing all into one. Here's how it went:

Introduction/Hook: Students sit down on their carpet as Ms. Resendes reads a book about the seasons and how leaves change colors and fall off of the trees in autumn.

Making Connections: Ms. Resendes reminds the students that yester-day they each got to pick a leaf from outside. "Can anyone make a con-nection from the story they just read to the leaves that they picked up yesterday? Are the leaves all the same size or are they different? Why is that?" These were some of the questions she challenged the students with.

Modeling and Guided Practice: Ms. Resendes talks about how today they are going to measure their leaves and shows that they will be using different manipulatives to measure their leaves, like cubes and popsicle sticks. She models how to measure other objects with those items to give an example of how to measure. She also models how to record their find-ings after measuring their leaf.

Independent Practice: Students find a space in the room to measure their leaf with the items provided. Ms. Resendes tells them all to head to their tables and wait for her to say to begin so she can make sure everyone is where they are supposed to be.

"Arianna, go tip your Humpty. You started before I asked you to begin. You were not following directions."

What was that? Humpty? Who is Humpty and why is he being tipped. I watched as Arianna walked over to the board and found the Humpty Dumpty with her name on it and tipped it to the side. Inside, I wanted to laugh because this was really funny watching an egg on the board being turned sideways, but I thought better in this situation. Arianna looked sad, but more importantly, Humpty looked like he was in trouble.

Students work diligently for several minutes measuring and recording their findings, while the teacher and teacher assistant monitor the room and ask thought-provoking questions while the students work.

Writing Integration: Students write down a sentence (with proper capitalization and punctuation) explaining the size of their leaf based on the number of sticks or cubes they used to measure it.

Analysis: The class returns to the carpet and discusses what they found when measuring their leaves. Ms. Resendes holds up two leaves that are about the same size, but one student found it was four blocks, while another found it was eight blocks. How could that be?*

Wrap-up: The class discusses any other observations they made while measuring and rehashed the stages of a leaf, the four seasons …

"Arianna, go get your Humpty. You are not paying attention." Oh-oh!

Man, this was not Arianna's day. Her Humpty was already half-way to an omelet. Arianna remorsefully got her Humpty off of the board and put it on Ms. Resendes' desk. Ms. Resendes never skipped a beat, however, and continued talking to the class without disrupting the flow of the lesson. I watched as Arianna sat back at her carpet square and welled up a tear in her eye. She wiped it away and finished the lesson by paying closer attention and even contributing to the class.

Some teachers would have stopped class and made a large ordeal about Arianna not paying attention or not following directions. This is not helping anyone. When you give a consequence, give it and move on. Do not allow the student time to react or argue. Whether you use Humpty, a clip, a color system, sticky notes, frogs, magical goats, or whatever else you decide upon, be consistent and establish clear and concise expectations with the students.

Arianna knew the expectations and rules of her class. Of course, she was not happy she had to remove her Humpty since it meant that she would receive a note home that day that said her Humpty had been turned into scrambled eggs (I doubt the note actually says that), but she realized she had not met the expectations of her teacher. Ms. Resendes sets those high expectations from day one and maintains them by utilizing her behavior management system and ensuring the students understand why they receive a consequence.

In case you're wondering the answer to "How could that be?" the students figured out that some measured the leaf horizontally while other measured it vertically, which would lead to measurements being different even though the leaves were about the same size. Are you smarter than a kindergartner?

What CAN you do? First and foremost, establish a behavior management system. It doesn't matter so much what it looks like as much as it matters how you utilize it. If it just takes up wall space, you have lost a valuable opportunity to make your life easier. Establishing a system in your class where students receive consequences for infractions of the rules provides order and understanding. Students like to know that there are rules, and while it is not enjoyable being on the receiving end of the consequence, they are more inclined to accept it if they know it is a fair and maintained system.

25.
You CAN ...
Put Yourself in Your Students' Shoes (or iPhones)

I took Stephanie, a fifth-grade student I was working with on academics, out to eat at Wendy's after we had just spent several hours studying for a big test in another class. We were both worn out, so we decided to take a break. One of my eighth graders had convinced me the week before to download this game called *Temple Run* on my iPhone because he said it was the best game ever. Well, if it was the best game ever, how could I pass that once-in-a-lifetime opportunity up?

I downloaded it and quickly gained respect for Indiana Jones because it is not easy jumping over bridges, sliding under fire, and outrunning flesh eating demons. In a nutshell, I stunk at it.

This does not come as much of a surprise to be honest. When I was younger, my brother Marc and I used to go over our neighbor Jason's house and played *Blades of Glory* on his Nintendo. For those not familiar, *Blades of Glory* was the most engaging 16-bit hockey game ever created. When two players fought, the entire game paused and you threw punches in basically slow motion. The puck looked more like a blackened bagel. The players slid down the ice as if they were, in fact, flying. But hey, it was all we had and it gave us something to do on rainy days.

The funny thing is I never really enjoyed playing the game. When I did play, I would get demolished by Marc or Jason, so I basically promoted myself to the "game advisor" on the sideline. As I grew older, I subsequently failed at other gaming systems when I gave them a shot. Game Boy, Genesis, Game Cube, Play Station—I played them all and found myself on the losing end of any game put in front of me.

Flash forward to today and now I can download and lose at games on my phone. Gotta love technology! So I now have *Temple Run* on my phone, and I was jumping into trees and being eaten by demons on a regular basis.

As Stephanie was trying to show me how to play this highly-addictive game on my phone, I was getting frustrated. I was trying to sweep left, jump, and slide simultaneously, and it was a disaster. But just minutes before, I was asking Stephanie to define and isolate variables, use the order of operations, and justify computation, something she struggled with.

I began putting two and two together in my head and realized it is exasperating not being able to do something that someone else can do. While I realized early on that video games were my Achilles' heel, since I never had to take a formal assessment or be graded on my gaming abilities, I had never faced the consequences of not being good at them.

The reality is math and other content areas do get tested, and students who struggle academically do get tired of losing in the game of test scores. Being put into a maddening experience by playing *Temple Run* with Stephanie made me remember that patience and relentless practice is necessary in order to grow and achieve. As her teacher, it was my job to continue to push her in her academics, and as my student, I charged her with the job of pushing me in my gaming skills. We would push each other and make each other stronger.

As I conduct workshops around the country, I often put teachers in the role of the student to ensure that they understand the pressure, and sometimes discomfort, that our students experience. I emphasize that it is good to feel uneasiness, as this is the way in which we develop our abilities. It is equally important to know ways in which to overcome adversity and jump hurdles that inevitably will get in our way of achievement.

One of my favorite ways to demonstrate this is to hold an impromptu debate during my workshop focused on rigor. I explain that twenty-first century skills involve being a quick thinker, a good listener, and an acute analyzer. Employers want workers who can solve problems, come up with solutions, and find ways to challenge the status quo in order to make change. Through debate, students can develop all of these skills in an engaging and purposeful manner.

I first call for any volunteers in the room. Usually I get someone who will step up and take one for the team. I explain that we are going to engage in a debate. But not just any debate, an impromptu debate. Neither the volunteer nor I have any idea about what we're going to discuss.

I pull up the CNN.com homepage and scroll down to their headlines section. I ask the participant to choose the U.S., World, or Politics heading. After that, I then choose an article from under that heading that looks like it would be a good topic to debate. After choosing the article, I read the first few paragraphs to ensure that the debaters and the audience have a general understanding of the context of the article. From there, I ask the audience to help come up with a debate topic stemming from the article. Once agreed upon, I allow the participant to choose which side he or she wants to argue for. I then receive the other side.

I always have the person I am debating start out the debate. Like clockwork, the person will stand in one place and rattle off a couple of thoughts on the subject. I then go into full presenter mode:

"Good morning, my name is Adam Dovico, and I am here today to convince you that the United States needs to remove itself from the happenings in North Korea. For too long the United States has been the keeper of the world, and this is yet another showcase example of stepping into other people's business. South Korea, while a friend of the U.S., needs to come to the realization that they are a sovereign nation and 'big brother' cannot always be there to save them ..."

All the while as I am saying this, I am moving about the audience, making strong eye contact, and using emotion in my words to convey my message. And the result …

Inevitable laughter.

I have done hundreds of impromptu debates in these workshops, and every time the audience chuckles as I begin because they immediately see the difference between the usually stoic participant and my opening. My opponent will usually catch on to the tactics I am using to engage my audience and adapt, just as I would expect my students to.

The most valuable piece is the conversation afterwards with the audience. We discuss the importance of modeling good debate, just as you would model how to perform an experiment, fill in a bubble, or stand in a straight line. In order to model, though, one must feel what it is like to debate, which is why I always encourage teachers to be the ones to do the modeling. Find another adult, or take a strong student, and debate a topic that you are discussing in class. In the end, you will see that the students pick up tricks and performance skills just by watching.

It can be intimidating, nerve-wrecking, and downright scary to go in front of a class and debate. For some students, it is the first time they have been in front of an audience. The student may not be a quick thinker or have much background knowledge. That is why it is so important to give opportunities for these students to practice and refine their skills.

In Bristol, TN (NASCAR country), one of the most talented teachers I have witnessed firsthand teaches sixth-grade math. Math is not just about finding answers in Mr. Laoo's class, but discovering how they came to that answer, why their answer does or doesn't makes sense, and uncovering alternative ways you can find that answer. As I observe him, I see students enjoying math, feeling comfortable with having an incorrect answer because they know that is how they improve. The students support each other by holding discussions and debates on ways in which they are solving problems. Most importantly, he never gives up on a student. When he chooses a student to answer a question, he sticks with him until the end. There is a no opt-out standard in the classroom, and by doing this, he is

Awesome

holding each student accountable for his or her learning. Mr. Laoo has put himself in their shoes and has found ways to help those students so that they do not get frustrated, but rather motivated to become better math students. Magnificent stuff!

Mr. Laoo, sixth-grade math teacher.

I want to close with a story about Lauren. Lauren came to me in fifth grade as a sweet young lady. She was as polite as can be and would do anything in her power to avoid being called on in class. I had taught her brother the year before, so I knew the family and knew Lauren even before she was in my class. It was my goal to break this streak of silence she had gotten away with for years.

It was the first formal debate of the school year in my class. I had modeled what it looks like, and we had talked about various tricks and maneuvers you could use if you got stuck during the debate. To be fair, I

113

drew popsicle sticks with the students' names on them out of my jar for who would come up first to debate. Low and behold, Lauren was chosen first to go up against Shawl.

Shawl opened up the debate and got the interaction moving. Over to Lauren … silence. Shawl interjected again and continued the flow of debate (as I taught the kids to do if your partner cannot think of anything to say). Since this bought Lauren some time to think, surely she would have something to say. Back over to Lauren … silence again. But not only do we have silence now, but tears began flowing down her face.

Oh boy. I had to make one of those quick teacher decisions. Do I let her stay up on stage and continue crying or just end it now?

I made her stay. Not only did I make her stay, but I gave her an F on her debate. I emailed her parents to give them the unraveling of events, and they completely supported me since we had built a great relationship from the year before.

The next week, guess who I purposefully called up to debate? While she did not have much to say again, she did not cry. Every time I made her debate that fifth-grade year, she improved. It was wonderful to watch.

But it was not as wonderful as watching her the next year during Staff Appreciation Night. In front of over three hundred students, parents, faculty, and friends, Lauren gave the opening monologue to welcome everybody to the event. She spoke with confidence and poise and delivered a perfect speech.

I walked over to Lauren and her mom after the event, and we talked about that first debate. We laughed about it, but inside I had to fight back a tear because I was so proud of how far she had come in such a short amount of time.

I want you to take a moment and think about the Lauren or Stephanie in the class, or the workplace, and what you can do for them to develop knowledge, skills, and confidence. Push that individual to go beyond their comfort zone and show that you believe in them with your words and actions. That's how we achieve results.

114

What CAN you do? Think about what it feels like to struggle at something, even if it is not academically related, as you work with your students. Those coping skills and words of encouragement are needed as you help people become less scared of their weaknesses. Demonstrate patience, understanding, and practical advice as you lead students through the process of becoming stronger students, presenters, thinkers, and citizens.

Coping skills
Words of encouragement
Demonstrate patience
understanding & practical
advice as you lead students
through process

26.
You CAN ...
Use Data

I am a numbers person, I always have been. I enjoy looking at data trends, making graphs, and analyzing numbers. I know some of you are getting a headache right now just reading this, but I personally find it interesting.

Teaching is a funny profession when it comes to data. Because we deal with human capital, at times we use our heart to make decisions rather than what the numbers and facts are telling us. Teachers sometimes get frustrated when decisions get passed down from the top that are based on research and data, rather than what we consider to be humanitarian or compassion.

It was the start of the school year at our pre-planning meeting, and the teachers finally received the highly-anticipated class roster! Who would be in my fifth-grade class? All of the fourth-grade teachers came running over and wanted to tell me about this kid and that kid. You could see wry smiles when they saw certain names, kind of like, "Have fun with him!"

There was one name that no one was familiar with. Her name was Briana, and I found out from our registrar that she just moved here from South Africa during the summer. I met Briana and her family at Back-to-School night and they were simply lovely. I asked her about her previous school and life in South Africa, and I felt a great bond with her family already.

School started the next day, and we jumped into content to shake off the summer cobwebs. As expected, most of the kids had to be refreshed with some of the concepts and skills from fourth grade, but Briana just sat there blankly. She frankly had no idea what she was looking at on the paper.

I closely monitored her over the next few days and realized that it wasn't getting better. I called her mom and asked her about any test scores or anything that she had from Africa. She said that all she had was some old workbooks that her class used. I looked at them the next day. The work she was doing in fourth grade was basically second- and third-grade work here in the U.S. I also found out that she had actually only completed half a year in fourth grade since their school year started in January.

All of the pieces were coming together, but I did not want to see the big picture. Briana was as polite and sweet as could be, and I knew that I would be able to help her catch up to the rest of her classmates. With the support of my administration, we had her entered into the student referral process just to make sure there were no learning issues. As a team, we would analyze her work and closely monitor her learning for a period of time. As it turned out, there were no learning issues, but it was once again confirmed that she was just not ready for fifth grade based on the content she had learned in Africa.

When I sat down with the principal, assistant principal, and literacy coordinator, they asked me what I wanted to do. Do I keep her in my class or put her back in fourth grade? I had all of the artifacts in front of me. I had the numbers to support having her do another year in fourth grade.

And I used my heart rather than my head. I kept Briana in my class for that year and she struggled as one would have assumed. She did show occasional growth and she maintained a decent work ethic, but an extra year in fourth grade would have made a tremendous difference.

At the end of the year, the family moved to another part of town, and from what I was told, she ended up doing another year in fifth grade. I look back now and regret not being smarter about my decision making. If I had used the numbers in front of me and realized that her deficiencies could have been made up in fourth grade, she would have been more successful that year.

The process of keeping data and analyzing it on a regular basis is not an easy one for teachers. When you take into account all of the duties that teachers are tasked with, data usually gets put to the backburner in many cases. In reality, data can and should drive the instruction and decisions being made in your classroom.

A good principal will provide time and opportunities for teachers to meet and discuss data from not only state assessments, but local assessments, informal and formal classroom assessments, attendance, discipline, and benchmark testing. If the school has an instructional coach, it is usually their job to lead this charge, and a strong instructional coach will help teachers compile and utilize their data in a helpful manner.

At one school I worked at all staff members utilized data notebooks. Depending on your grade level, you were to keep various up-to-date data on your students. In my notebook, I kept the students' End of Grade test scores from fourth grade, local assessment results that we administered three times a year, Lexile scores (reading levels) that were done using STAR testing, attendance records, parent communication logs, and pre- and post-test results from inside my class.

Personally, I enjoyed keeping this notebook and compiling the data. I realized that not everyone was as excited as me, but we saw the purpose and we used it to drive our instruction. When I became an instructional coach later on at another school, I took this idea of data notebooks with me and implemented it at my new school.

Since it was a new concept and not all of the teachers were comfortable with it yet, I designed grade level data notebooks instead of individual ones. Along with my fellow instructional coach, we had grade levels keep up-to-date records with useful data that could drive decision making for their teaching.

Each Tuesday, at grade level meetings, I would work with each grade level on looking over the data and discussing what instructional practices could be brought in to help address various needs. For example, when third-grade teachers saw that their students were struggling with multiplication facts, we realized that the real deficit dated back to addition fluency, so I created math lab centers that allowed the kids to play games and do activities to practice their math facts in an engaging fashion. Over time, the teachers were able to track progress made in math fact fluency, and this became helpful when targeting students for remediation and tutoring during state testing time.

I have visited schools where they have dedicated an entire room or section of the office to nothing but data. Some schools focus their data display more as an entity; others choose to go student by student. Either way, this shows a dedication to employing data as a valuable tool to drive decision making.

At a middle school in St. Louis I visited, I was brought into the instructional coach's office to observe her data obsession. I was blown away! Now to some, this would be like a scene out of *A Beautiful Mind*, where there are codes connecting to letters connecting to numbers making cryptic messages, but to me, this was a work of art. On one wall was data related to learning objectives, broken down by student; on another wall were grade level benchmarks and testing results identifying below, meeting, and exceeding standards. And my favorite part, everything was color coded. Oh, she and I got along great the days I was there!

The instructional coach explained that all grade level planning was done in this room, and teams spent the first bit of planning once a week updating and analyzing the data to pinpoint areas of need for the students. She did say the teachers moaned and groaned at times by having to do it, but they had results to show growth in the targeted areas, so something was working.

At an elementary school in Charlotte, I was able to observe data walls that were strung across the office. No parents or visitors were permitted in this area, so it was private for staff, but it served as a motivational tool, as well. Because it showed classrooms by name, there was a bit of a competitive edge created when your class was not doing as well as the others. Now, before you ask, their numbers were based on growth and achievement, so it was a level playing ground for a class that had remediation versus gifted students. In talking to the teachers, they didn't mind the wall because it gave them a visual for something to work towards. The administration did an excellent job of rewarding teachers and classrooms that met goals and benchmarks, as well, so there were carrots on the end of the sticks for all involved.

What CAN you do? It can be difficult to make or accept decisions that go against your teacher's instinct, especially when it has to do with your students. Discussions based on fact and data hold value to stakeholders, and this should be the foundation behind what drives instruction in our classrooms and schools. Data notebooks can be an excellent starting point for maintaining and utilizing data. Collect items such as test scores, attendance records, parent communication, and researched practices to place into your notebook. These will come in handy when having discussions with your fellow teachers, administration, or parents concerning your instruction. Data walls and data rooms serve as excellent conversation starters when discussing where your students are academically and finding areas of focus in the learning. It is also important to note, using data and making decisions based on it does not mean your teaching has to be "boring." Instructional decisions and delivery are two distinct things. The strongest teachers excel at both.

Visual testing data Broken down into targeted areas

27.
You CAN ...
Learn in First Class

"Drum roll please ...

The next person selected will receive *the leather chair* for the entire next week."

For many years, this was my weekly ticket drawing grand finale. Students would earn tickets throughout the week for various reasons, and on Fridays we had ticket drawing time, where you could earn prizes, beloved Air Head candy, and the coveted leather chair.

In reality, it was a typical black leather office chair that you would find in any business, but since it was not the typical classroom chair, *and* I made a big deal out of it, *and* you had to earn the tickets to get chosen, *and* it was something everyone wanted, winning it was that much more special.

The rule was that you were permitted to sit in the chair any time you were in my classroom at your desk. You could not auction it off to another student or make trades for other things (I had to put that rule in after I saw Pokémon cards being exchanged for chairs). You could not roll around like it was a carnival ride, and if you fell over in it, you lost your chair rights for the rest of the week.

Overall, it was a huge success. The kids enjoyed winning the right to sit in it, and it gave me something to get the kids excited about.

When I began working at the Ron Clark Academy, my classroom was decorated in a travel theme. Thanks to Delta Air Lines, I was overflowing with old Delta Air Lines furniture and parts. My desk was an old ticket check-in counter, my supplies cabinet was an old beverage cart, my book shelf was an old overhead bin from a plane, and decorations included oxygen air masks, life vests, and an old cockpit door (which was unbelievably heavy). I also had several airplane seats that were mighty comfortable to sit in.

I decided that those would become my "first-class seating." Instead of a ticket drawing, I would use the airplane seats for my students who performed well on assessments or showed tremendous growth. I had three seats, so I could use my discretion as to who I wanted in them. Even though these were basic economy section airplane seats, it had the same power as the leather chair did. It was unique to a classroom, and the kids thought it was cool to sit in them.

When it came time to announce new first-class seating—which I tried to change up about once every one to two weeks—we would get the drum roll going, and we celebrated those students who would get to sit there. They made for great desks because these were all emergency exit row seats, which meant that their tray table was within the armrest, which was an adventure for some students to figure out how to use! I had to have a mini-lesson with my fifth graders each year on how to take the tray table out if you were in first-class seating.

The seats also still had their original belt buckles, and on the couple of occasions Charlie got to sit in first class, he always insisted on buckling his seat belt. This made it quite humorous when I called him up to debate one day and he forgot that he still had the belt on. You can imagine the result when he tried standing up and he got pulled right back into that seat!

Mr. Townsel, a phenomenal science teacher I worked with, had a similar idea with his "front-row seating." He also had extra comfortable chairs that his top scholars earned based on their assessments. They got to be right up front and center in the classroom. For some students that might be a punishment to have to sit right up front, but not with Mr. Townsel. It was an honor and privilege to be up there, and that is because he presented the seats in a manner where it is truly special to be in that spot.

It was always a challenge to keep your "front-row seating," though, because Mr. Townsel made sure to point out that everyone was out to get those seats from you. This motivated the students currently in those seats to keep ahead of the curve, and for the other students to fight and claw their way to the top. It was a bit of a cat-and-mouse game, but in the end, all students are challenging and motivating themselves to work harder. A great example of think smarter, not harder!

What CAN you do? You can purchase fancy looking chairs from consignment and second-hand stores at a fairly reasonable price. You can also ask around to see if friends or family are looking to get rid of old office chairs. They make for a great addition in your classroom. You can use them as an incentive, a prize, or earned reward to engage and motivate your students. Remember, the bigger deal you make out of it, and the more build up you have when announcing who gets to sit in the chair, the more special you have made it and the more excited the students will be.

28.
You CAN ...
Set the Pace

I observed a high school social studies lesson on the French Renaissance during a school visit. It was the first period of the day and many of the students looked lethargic from having to walk from the door to their desk. This daunting task surprisingly took some students several minutes. After the bell rang, students were still filing in towards their seats and sitting there without any materials. The teacher asked the students to take out their social studies book from under their seats and then direct their attention to the board. On the board, she wrote down ten words from a sheet of paper in her hands that were vocabulary for the lesson. She then instructed the students to find these words in the back of the social studies book and write down the definition in their notebook (for those who actually had one).

Five minutes pass ... most students still looking for a piece of paper, pen, or social studies book.

Fifteen minutes pass ... teacher sitting at her desk while some students gave up on their search of needed items.

Thirty minutes pass ... I'm running out of things to observe because no one is doing anything.

At thirty-four minutes she arises from the desk and acquires their attention to go over the words. It was a forty-eight minute block. Do you see a problem here?

I was dumbfounded. A teacher just had students spend over two-thirds of her class period copying definitions from the back of the book. The kicker for me was that most of the students didn't even do the assignment. As they discussed the words, the student responding to the definition of *Renaissance* gave a personalized definition: "A time period in history." That's verbatim.

Afterwards, I debriefed with the teacher and asked her about her teaching style and how she feels she does teaching the standards. She admitted that she usually does not have time to teach the content that she wants to teach.

Shocking.

I politely walked through several concerns and discussed that having the students simply copy the definitions out of the back of the book— which they did not even do—was not going to help them learn about the French Renaissance. We came up with better ways to include vocabulary in the content in a more engaging and meaningful way.

Her other concern was that the students work too slowly, and they move at even a more lackluster pace. Can't argue there! I turned it back around, though, and asked her to reflect on her pacing. Recognizing the need for some scaffolding, I asked her about the start to her class. *How come the students did not have any materials out when the bell rang? How come the words they were going to use were not already on the board?*

Then we talked about her pacing during the class. *Could she have used a timer during the vocabulary? Was there a way to create a sense of urgency in the classroom through modeling?*

The pace of the class is set *by the teacher.* The teacher is solely responsible for the pace in which the kids are moving. When I talk to teachers who say their kids are moving too slowly, 99 times out of 100 the teacher is moving even slower. You *can* set the pace by establishing strong classroom management procedures and expectations.

To describe, I look no further than Ms. Stallings' eighth-grade language arts classroom. I had the opportunity to observe Ms. Stallings a couple of times. I'll be honest, I was not blown away by her the first time, but her principal said I needed to check her out again. I'm so glad I did.

I made sure to get to the class before the students entered so I could see the beginning of class. As the students entered, even before the bell, they had clear directions written on the board for what to do. They were to put their bags down, take out a pencil, and begin going around the room to respond to quotes that were taken from *The Hunger Games*, which they had just completed reading as a class.

As the bell rang, most students were already in the room walking around hard at work. After five minutes, a timer went off and she asked the students to return to their seats. She greeted them with a good afternoon, and then began going around the room to the different quotes that were on the wall to have discussions about how people responded to the quotes. She challenged students on their responses and held brief impromptu debates on differing opinions that existed. Afterwards, she led the students into a follow-up activity where they would now be working in pairs on finding specific quotes from the book that aligned with an idea that they selected. For example, the students would have to find a quote that demonstrated "love" or "vengeance." All the while, the students eagerly participated and remained engaged and focused on the task at hand.

Before they began this second activity, the students lined up to go to the bathroom. This was the first block after lunch, so naturally, many of them needed a bathroom break. Every student, whether they needed the restroom or not, lined up at the door and entered the hallway; within two minutes, every student was back in their chair. I thought I was dreaming. I have never seen students move with such urgency and purpose, low and behold eighth graders!

The students continued their activity as the teacher monitored the room, stopping off at various groups to not only see what they were writing down, but challenging them to think about why they chose it. It was time for me to go on to another observation, but before I did, I felt compelled to say something to the class—which is a first and only time for me as an observer.

I told them that they were by far and away the most impressive middle school students I had observed in my travels. Not only did they respectfully interact with each other, but they understood and abided by the procedures in the class. I said that as I travel around, it is only because of the teacher that something like this could happen, so I encouraged them to say thank you to Ms. Stallings for being their teacher and setting up a classroom that was rigorous, engaging, and productive. I could tell that they were proud of themselves for receiving this type of compliment, but even happier for Ms. Stallings because the students knew it was because of her high expectations and classroom culture that this class was receiving the compliment.

As I compare these two classrooms that I have described, the difference for me came down to the pacing that the two teachers established in the classroom. While there were inevitably other variables that starkly differed, it was the pacing that stood as the largest divide. In the first room, the pace of the room did not require the students to move quickly, focus, or engage themselves because it was not an expectation that the teacher demonstrated. Ms. Stallings, on the other hand, established her routine long ago with her class, and that expectation was maintained through her ability to be prepared with her lesson and the materials to go along with it. Ms. Stallings' pacing enabled her students to be successful, and that is what all teachers should aim for.

What CAN you do? How are your students walking into class? Do they plod, resembling a funeral march? If so, why is it? Reflect on the pacing and sense of urgency that you present in the classroom. Be sure that the students know the expectation for when they walk into the classroom. Are they to take out a certain material? Look at the board for directions? Do a warm up problem? Ask yourself if your materials are ready each day and if they are engaging activities or simply busy work. The good teacher will establish routines and procedures that will allow the students to move with a sense of urgency; the great teacher will *demonstrate* the routines and procedures that move the students with a sense of urgency.

29.
You CAN ...
Videotape Yourself

My eighteen-month-old son Ryder has recently found a new hobby. He saw how daddy pressed a magical button on his iPhone, and all of a sudden, Ryder can see himself singing in the bathtub or falling asleep while eating dinner. I think he is finally figuring out that the baby in the video is him. He goes through a series of confusion, laughter, and embarrassment each time we watch them.

With a touch of my finger, I can record video, take pictures, and collect audio on my phone. Beyond that, I have flip cams, iPads, webcams, and any number of devices at my disposal. It seems like a no-brainer then that I would use this as a tool in my classroom.

By simply videotaping yourself in the classroom, you learn a lot about yourself as a teacher. Each time I use this reflection technique, I find something that I want to improve upon. Whether it is my positioning while teaching, who I am calling on, questions I am asking, or my transition times, I am able to analyze my film in order to reflect and adjust.

This should not be unfamiliar to those of you who have played sports in high school or college. What does any good athlete do to improve? Watch the tapes!

Tiger Woods, one of the all-time great golfers, has managed to reinvent his golf swing multiple times. For anyone who has golfed, it's hard to get one swing to work, nonetheless three of them, and still win as much as he has. In an April 2011 *Golf Digest* article, Jaime Diaz talks about Tiger's coaches having him watch video of the evolution of his swing in order to find ways to improve it. One coach even had Tiger watch video of his swing in high school, "as if the future can be found in the beginning." Can the same rules apply to teaching? Let's take a look.

Over your teaching career you will likely adopt various teaching styles, possibly depending on the grade level you are teaching, the demographics of the school, or the content you are responsible for. There will be some mechanics and idiosyncrasies that are just inherent to you, but you develop new habits over time. It may turn out that something you did long ago may serve you well years down the line, much like Tiger Woods realized in his career.

Many of us may not have video of ourselves teaching from years ago, since it was not as easy back then to obtain, set up, and tape ourselves with bulky cameras and equipment. Times have changed! With technology readily accessible and easy to use, setting up the camera on the back shelf, or with a simple tripod, can be done within seconds.

The reflection piece is the most valuable element of this process. Having an administrator, academic coach, or co-worker sit down and watch the video with you can be awkward (I personally cringe when I hear myself on camera), but it's a necessary evil. Having a neutral party reflecting with you will add to the value of this introspective practice.

I sometimes videotape teachers when I observe classrooms so that we may review the tape and reflect afterwards. Here are common questions I probe teachers with after reviewing the tape:

- What was a moment during the lesson you believe captivated the students, so much so, that you had them eating out of the palm of your hand?
- What was a moment where you think you lost the students, either due to disengagement or confusion? What did you do to correct it or what could you have done?
- What percentage of the students do you think you made eye contact with?
- How do you feel your positioning was in regards to engaging the entire class?
- What was the highlight of the lesson for you?
- Name one thing that you would change if you did this lesson again right now.

I also have the teacher keep track of the students who answer a question with a simple tally sheet of the class roster. The purpose of this is for the teacher to see who is being called on and not being called on. In the heat of teaching, it is sometimes hard to remember who you have called on or trying to identify students who need to participate more. There is, of course, extra pressure when there is someone else in the room or a video camera rolling. This is why it is helpful to regularly participate in this type of reflective practice. Videotaping and reflecting on a frequent basis will allow you to be more comfortable not only teaching while taping, but identifying ways in which you can improve as a teacher.

One other benefit that you will find from this practice is student accountability. I was able to catch a whole lot of things that my students were doing that I missed while I was teaching by watching back the tape. In some cases, I would show it to the child and hypothetically ask what their parents would have thought if they saw the tape, because as easy as it is to press the delete button, it's just as easy to press the email video button. Usually, I don't have any more problems from that child after that.

What CAN you do? If you have a smart phone, tablet, flip cam, or anything else that takes video, use it to grow as an educator. If possible, have a co-worker or friend do the videotaping, that way the camera can follow you around the room. Otherwise, set up the camera on a table or shelf so that you can be seen, but your students are in the screen shot, as well. After videotaping, watch the video back and take notes on things that you did well and areas that you want to improve upon. Try to get another person to come watch it with you so that you get additional feedback.

30.
You CAN ...
Create Mini-Me's

Remember in *Austin Powers* when Dr. Evil introduced Mini-Me as his diabolical half-sized side-kick? Well, in my own unusual way I always envisioned creating my version of Mini-Me in the classroom. I have no intentions on world domination or earning (make sure you say this in your best Dr. Evil voice) *"ONE MILLION DOLLARS!"* but I certainly would not object to producing a student to be someone who loves learning about history and thinks hard math problems are cool.

It is a tall order to be a role model for a group of children. We must be careful of each step we take because people are watching. There is no faster way to perk up and break into a cold sweat than to hear, "Mr. Dovico!" as you are walking down the cereal aisle at the grocery store, wondering what parent you are about to encounter. While it can be a bit inconvenient to have a parent-teacher conference while standing in line to check out, I have never shied away from interacting with my students and families in and out of the classroom. Personally, I believe it makes us more human. I remember seeing my teachers around town when I was younger and being in awe. *I thought they lived at school!*

As teachers, we have magical powers to influence in ways that parents do not. When mom or dad says something is important, it can go in one ear and out the other, but when Mr. Dovico says it, it's going to happen! This is why I get frustrated when my son does not listen to me—I'm just dad to him!

I was teaching my gifted fifth-grade language arts class about citation formats (APA, MLA, Chicago) so that they could become familiar with several types, since I told them that they will find teachers have preferences of one over another. I happened to have my old *A Writer's Reference* by Diana Hacker book with me from my college days. Mind you, this is before you could go online and have websites create the entire citation for you, so I had to teach the kids the old fashion way about creating a citation by finding the title, author, publisher, publishing city, date, etc.

I'm not sure how it happened, but they thought this was the most fun thing in the world. They could not get enough of citations, and more specifically, this writer's reference book. They were obsessed with it. And then I showed them that there were grammar rules, revision rules, word choice suggestions, syntax rules, and document designs in this book, too! You would have thought that they had just found the Holy Grail!

Now it might have helped that I built this book up to be the Mecca of college reads, but whatever it takes, right? While I hoped that the kids would remember some of the rules we learned with citing text, never in my wildest dreams would I have thought that the introduction of this manual would lead me to writing this email to a parent:

From: *Adam Dovico*
To: *Donna*
Sent: *1/2/2008 6:16:25 PM*
Subject: *Bailey*

Hey there, happy New Year! I thought you'd like to know Bailey has provided me with one of my all-time favorite funny moments today ...
Bailey: "Mr. Dovico, guess what I got for Christmas?"

Me: *"What's that?"* (in my head I'm thinking a new video game, clothes, money— like the other kids who told me what they got for Christmas)

Bailey: (opening up her bag with a gigantic smile) *"A Writer's Reference book!"*

That is an excellent gift from Santa, as I told Bailey— that will help her through the next 10+ years of schooling!
Have a good one!!

Mr. Adam Dovico

Her reply ...

Mr. Dovico (aka Santa's Helper),

Thanks for making my Christmas shopping so easy!!! (okay, a little expensive, but I guess it was cheaper than the iPod she wanted!) We're glad she made you laugh and we appreciate you taking the time to share your "Bailey" moment with us! She was determined to get that book and I'm sure she will use it because she is so passionate about writing! You have made such an impact on her in the short time that she has been with you – thank you!!! She truly loves your class and you have gained the status of "favorite teacher"! Keep up the great work!

Happy New Year!

Donna

Mini-me creation complete! I can see the rewrite of the Mariah Carey song now: *All I want for Christmas is* ~~You~~ *(A Writer's Reference)*. In all seriousness, this was a pretty cool moment for me as a teacher. To see that I had created enough excitement about this book that it caused one of my girls to beg her mom to get it for her for Christmas, is somewhat remarkable.

It turns out that after some kids in the class found out that Bailey had gotten the book, it became the hip thing to beg your mom for. I had another three or four kids in the class that were walking around with their already oversized book bags now stuffed with a writing manual. They would pull those suckers out each and every time they wrote and learned how to check grammar rules and use proper citations.

As I peered over this unique bunch of kids, I kept thinking, "This was me." When I was younger, I would get mad at my parents over whatever thing kids typically get mad at their parents for. I would "run away" from home when I got mad, but never made it further than my front porch. I suppose I thought that was far enough. Whenever I did this, though, I would bring a box of crackers (since you have to eat) and my dictionary, because clearly no runaway child is complete without a dictionary.

My parents, trying not to laugh too hard, would let me go about my business of being mad and sitting on the front porch with my crackers and dictionary. I would sit there with a pout on my face and read the words and definitions in the book. After twenty or so minutes, I returned from my excursion a calmer (and smarter) boy.

Another exciting Mini-Me moment for me came during Teacher Appreciation week at the Ron Clark Academy. The parents had put together a fancy looking newspaper called "RCA Times," which was a tribute to the teachers and staff of the school. Next to my picture, Mariah wrote:

I really love competing for the Debate Belt! It is so cool. I love to wear it because it lets the whole school and all of our guests know we won a debate! I also love current events. Now, I go to my friend's house and they want to watch cartoons and I want to watch CNN. I think they are so immature at times. Who really chooses cartoons over CNN?

Wow! That's all I could say when I read that. I converted a ten year old over to the dark side! By sharing my love of news and what's going on in the world, I was now having conversations with my students that few adults could hold with each other. Interestingly enough, when we had visiting teachers at the Ron Clark Academy, the kids would often try to engage with the guests in conversation about what was going on in the world. On numerous occasions the kids came up to me afterwards shocked that the adults had no idea what they were talking about.

I think I can sum this up by saying, I love learning. It was clear from a young age that even in my lowest of moments I was looking to learn. Some habits stay with you into adulthood and are subconsciously exhibited as we work with others. For me, this love of learning comes out when I am with my students, and if creating a mini-me means producing students who share the same passion as me, I'm willing to take on that responsibility.

What CAN you do? Think about your passions as an individual. Perhaps it's a love of sports, animals, or machines. Take that with you as you enter the classroom and share it with your students. While the reality is there are many negative influences that our kids are exposed to each day, they also learn from the positive influences, as well, and you can be that person in a child's life. Create your mini-me by recognizing a child who shares a similar passion as you and encouraging them to continue that drive by supporting and being a role model for them.

31.
You CAN ...
Informally Assess

We've all been in those moments when you just step back and say, "What in the world just happened?" At first, you want to blame someone else or make an excuse, but perhaps it's just easiest to reflect and think about what could have been done better. Please find on the next page an epic fail in teaching content from early on in my career. This was an essay test that we gave as a grade level to all of the students on the causes of the American Revolutionary War. Overall, the students did not do all that well, and after reading this particular essay, I realized "Houston, we have a problem."

Instructions: Using your scavenger hunt as your resource, write a short essay on the causes of the American Revolutionary War. Do not just give a list of definitions, but tell the story about the events that led up to the first shots being fired at Lexington and Concord ("the shot heard around the world") in paragraph form.

Be sure to use the following words or terms in your essay: French and Indian War, Proclamation of 1763, Sugar Act, Stamp Act, Boston Massacre, Boston Tea Party, Intolerable Acts, First Continental Congress, and Second Continental Congress.

The Boston tea party was about. this bad boys who dump all the tea in to harber which is Massisirees river and they had no tea left. because the indeins probibly did not now how to make tea brick then cause they did'nt halve the ingestis to make tea back then. but now we have that stuff today. but in the old days. they didn't but now we will not forget the Boston tea party. Now we have different kinds of tea today like sweet and unsweet teas. I like the sweet tea because it is really sweet with a lot of surger in it. My mom like's the unsweet which has no surger but just a little bit of surger in the unsweet tea.

This is the translation (sort of) for this essay:

The Boston tea party was about. this bad boys who dumped the tea in to harbar which is Massisherses river and they had no tea left. because the indeins probably did not new how to make tea back then cause they didn't have the ingeetients to make tea back then. but now we have that stuff today. but in the old days they didn't. but now we will not forget the Boston tea party. Now we have different kinds of tea today like the sweet tea because it is really sweet with alot of surger in it. My mom like's the unsweet whitch has no surger but just a little bit of surger in the unsweet tea.

So I'll ask you, what would you do here? There are writing issues, content issues, and apparently tea issues for mom. I've asked people this question before and usually, I have to first wait until they're done laughing to answer. Then I hear a variety of answers from "reteach the content" to "just move on" to "I don't know where to begin." I personally believe that I could have avoided this situation all together if I had done a better job of informally assessing the students before giving this test.

Often we are left with simply trying to get through the content in order to get to the quiz or test. This leaves few opportunities to see if the kids actually understand the material. As I developed as a teacher, I implemented more frequent, quick ways to informally assess the students in order to know whether they were ready or not to take a quiz or a test. I developed rapid games and activities that would become fairly popular with my students, and eventually other teachers, as I began doing educator training. Here are a few of my favorite games that can be used for informal assessment:

1) Dice Game: This is played between two or three people. To start, each student gets a sheet that has a series of things to be solved. For example, multiplication fact sheet, a blank periodic table, a

series of multiple choice questions, etc. Each group needs one number cube. The group decides who will start out with the cube. The person (or people) who do not have the cube will then have a writing utensil. When the teacher says, "GO!" the students with the pen or pencil begin filling in the answers. The student with the number cube begins rolling it, trying to get whatever number you designate as "the magic number." I always use six because it's easy to remember, but you can choose any number you want. Once they get a six, they yell, "SIX!" and the person who had the cube passes it to his or her partner, and the person who had the writing utensil does the same. If there are three people in a group, the number cube just goes between the three individuals. The game goes back and forth until someone finishes or you simply want to end the game. At the end of the game, collect the sheets and take a look to see if the students truly understood what you were aiming to assess them on. In the case from the essay above, I would have played this game by having the students list the causes of the Revolutionary War. If I saw too many sheets that came back with incorrect or insufficient answers (which is likely what would have happened in this case), I could have gone back and retaught the causes.

2) Minute to Win It: This idea comes from Mr. Padgett (though influenced by the television game show), a magnificent teacher in South Carolina, who I had the chance to observe teach fourth grade. At one point during his class, he instructed the students to clear off their desks. After the students did so, he told them all to get their pencils in position. The kids knew exactly what that meant, and you could also see a smile appear on many of their faces like they knew what was coming. Mr. Padgett then had the students pass around a math fact sheet. The students placed it in front of them, but did not start working. Without having to say a word, all of the students' hands went into the air and the teacher walked over to his Smart Board. He opened the YouTube video and clicked it. The video's

voice then says, "The game begins in three, two, one," and then a blaring air horn rings out. For the next sixty seconds, a heart-wrenching, blood-curdling music plays, and all the while the students are vigorously working on their fact sheet. At the end of the minute, another horn sounds and all of the students' hands simultaneously went back up to end the game. Mr. Padgett instructed the students to pass the sheets in and that concluded the game. This entire process only took three minutes. I simply loved the concept of using this as an informal assessment game, where the students are working under pressure, forcing them to focus and think. I learned that this game was used frequently in the class, and Mr. Padgett kept track of the number correct that the students got so they could monitor their growth throughout the year.

3) Snow Ball Fight: If you are prone to high blood pressure, or simply get nervous when kids start moving about the classroom, this game may not be for you! The Snow Ball fight has all the makings for complete chaos, which is why it is imperative that you are confident in your classroom management before engaging in this crusade. To begin, divide your class up into two groups. I either come up with funny names for the sides or let the kids do it. Draw an imaginary line down the middle of the room and establish strict boundaries that no student may go during the game. For instance, behind the teacher's desk, under the computers, or any other potentially hazardous location. Each student is to have with them a sheet of paper and a pen. You may allow students fifteen seconds to turn a chair or desk in order to make a "fortress" just for fun. No stacking chairs on desks! When you say, "Go!" each student writes down an answer to a problem or an example from whatever you are reviewing. After they write this down, they take the piece of paper, crumble it up, and toss it like a snowball to the other side of the room. Students should be looking out to get snowballs as they land near them. They are to open up a snowball that they find and write the next answer or a new fact on the

sheet of paper. They then crumble it back up and throw it across again. This goes on for about ninety seconds, after which you call a "Cease fire!" and everyone returns to their desk, likely sweaty and panting. The teacher collects the sheets (which are going to look like they went through the washing machine) and will be able to decipher the degree to which the students have an understanding of the content. For example, if I saw that George Washington's election as President was a cause of the Revolutionary War, I know there was more teaching to be done!

All of these games are high energy, and ensure a sense of urgency in the classroom, which is what any good teacher is going to desire. The students do not need to be reminded to start the game, and oftentimes, they are begging to play it more. If the students enjoy playing the games, this provides you with a carrot on a stick as students desire to play them again.

What CAN you do? Find quick, engaging means to frequently informally assess your students. Students need to interact with material in order for it to be retained, and if it is done in what they consider a fun way, they are likely to participate more. There are many games and activities like the ones above that can be done in any classroom at any level. Collaborate and share with fellow teachers to come up with other learning games that can be used to ensure that your students are ready to be formally assessed.

32.
You CAN ...
Show Appreciation Towards Each Other

Appreciation can be shown in many ways. Some choose to give monetary gratitude, as in tipping. Others choose to give gifts or a verbal "thank you." Whatever the means, it is important that we show appreciation. This simple act can build stronger relationships and establish a positive climate. When all individuals each dedicate themselves to better the environment they work in, change can happen!

There was no one better at this than one of my former principals, Tisha Greene. Tisha had the ability to show people how much she cared about them, and how much she appreciated their hard work on a consistent basis, no matter how busy she was. I was the recipient of her kind acts on a number of occasions, and I kept some of her cards as a reminder to continue this act towards others. Here is the text from a handwritten card I got on my birthday:

Adam,
I knew when Beverly called me, I had a rare opportunity to work with some-
one I see as an up and coming leader in CMS and education. You are fabu-
lous and your constant positivity is refreshing. I know you will be excellent
wherever you go.

With heartfelt gratitude,

Tisha Greene

If that can't warm up your day, I don't know what can. This small act of kindness is what made me want to work even harder for Tisha and for the school.

Acts like this can also become infectious. After receiving notes from Tisha, I wrote notes of appreciation to other teachers for what they were doing in the classroom and around the school. Can you imagine a school where all staff members are showing appreciation of each other on a consistent basis?

We also established a system at the school to reward teachers and staff for their hard work. When a member of the administrative team (which I was a part of at this school) saw a staff member that should be recognized for excelling in their job, we provided them with Falcon Funds (our mascot was a falcon). Recognition could come from an excellent lesson, covering a duty for someone, or going above and beyond for the school. This play money could then be used at the end of the month to bid on prizes that the administrative team accumulated, such as classroom decorations, free lunches, gift cards, etc. The teachers loved it and it lifted staff morale and unity.

I did professional development training at a school in Georgia on one of their teacher workdays. At the end of the day, the principal said they had something for me. She proceeded to open up a website on the Smart

Board to reveal a series of sticky note like messages that thanked me for coming and saying what they enjoyed during the training. It was done on a program called Padlet (padlet.com), and it allows people to post messages on this interactive page. Any person can add a message to it by double-clicking on the screen, but the creator of the page does have administrative rights and can edit the page. I thought this was the neatest tool! I was so touched with the thoughtfulness that I keep it handy to look at whenever I'm feeling a bit worn out. I now share this tool with schools when I do training so perhaps they, too, can show appreciation in a unique way towards each other.

In my travels around the country, the climate of a school's staff (how happy is everyone) can typically be brought back directly to the administration. When I talk to teachers who feel protected, supported, and uplifted by their administration, that sentiment carries throughout the building. I observe teachers who are doing the same for their students and students who are doing it for each other. At the same time, schools that have administrators who the staff does not trust, that negativity and cynicism frequently permeates throughout every facet of the school.

Demonstrating appreciation is an easy way to build the trust and support of a staff. Writing a note, sending an email, providing breakfast in the morning, are all simple ways to build a positive climate in a school. As an administrator, you have immense influence and control over how your staff bonds and grows together.

What CAN you do? Time gets away from us. It is easy to use lack of it as an excuse as to why we didn't show more appreciation toward each other. Make it a point to thank someone, even if in the simplest of words, for what they are doing. When appreciation becomes a habit rather than a chore, attitudes change, behaviors change, and in the end, we are making the whole stronger.

33.
You CAN ...
Correct Behaviors
Immediately

It was a hot and humid Florida day (which I learned was frequently the case), and I drove around with a woman who was looking to start a school. We met with a gentleman who was a builder in the area, but also owned the building that she was looking to buy to house her school.

He had experience with starting schools, as he had been on the board of the school that currently sat in the building the woman was looking to buy. The school was shutting down at the end of the year, and the gentleman explained that, over the years, there had been any number of issues that can be looked back at now as what led to the closing of this school. Mismanagement, funding issues, and entitlement could have all been things easily addressed by the board at the time they were happening, but that did not always happen, as he explained, and as a result, the school had to close its doors.

The man then used a magnificent analogy to draw a comparison to this situation. He explained that a friend of the family who flew planes in World

War II once told him that as he flew across the Atlantic, when he drifted off course, he would immediately correct it so he remained on path, and in the end, he would arrive at his expected destination. If he had waited until the end of the flight to make the correction, he would have been far off course and not have had enough fuel to get him to where he wanted to go.

As I let this wrap around my brain, I, of course, drew this back to teaching, and I had one of those "a-ha" moments. When I go into classrooms that are off the chain, i.e., students are being disruptive, rude, or downright crazy, they did not arrive there overnight. These behaviors came from an accumulation of not "redirecting" them along the way. As a result, we have a student who is so far off course that it would take an immense amount of work to bring them to where we wanted them to be. Additionally at this point, the teacher is likely out of fuel and can't or won't even bother making the corrections after draining themselves along the way. Are you following me so far?

Let's also look at academics here. When a student in seventh grade has trouble reading a page in the textbook, this is not a problem that suddenly appeared. Once again, this is the sum of years of not making the corrections along the way.

If it is as easy as making just small corrections along the way, why do we still have students misbehaving in class and not performing well academically? I think most teachers will say that it is tough addressing behaviors or misunderstandings immediately when you have twenty plus other kids to also deal with. Can't argue there, but let's look at how good teachers still manage to do it.

I observed Ms. Bellow's third-grade classroom and quickly realized that this was not going to be my typical classroom observation. Ms. Bellow has gained the reputation of being able to work with any student, which in teacher language means she is good at dealing with the kids who many teachers label as "difficult." As a result, Ms. Bellow housed quite the assortment of students. As I watched her teach, I could not help but be inspired by her efforts.

While she was teaching about the importance of a strong topic sentence in your writing, she was simultaneously bringing a blanket from a closet to a student who needed it for his tactile disorder. Immediately after, but while still teaching, she was caringly putting her arm around a fidgety student who was getting angry because she would not let him go to the principal's office. The entire time she never took her eyes off the class and was smiling so big that no student would have noticed that she was doing literally fifteen things at once. She energetically taught her lesson, but made sure to address behaviors as they came up in a calm, smooth tone that never disrupted the flow of the lesson. As a result, the large population of kids who needed extra attention in Ms. Bellow's class were not only getting that individual attention they needed, but they were also still acquiring the content they needed to learn.

Mr. Fields is a high school science teacher. Honestly, he looks more like he could be a surfer or a basketball player, but appearances don't always tell the full story. Mr. Fields is a quick-witted, likeable guy who the kids would not dare challenge because they know that he can dish it out quicker than they could. Except Samuel. Samuel, I learned, loved to challenge Mr. Fields in whatever way possible. Samuel was sneaky—he could poke a pencil into the back of someone's neck faster than you could blink. Mr. Fields had his number, though, and could predict when Samuel was about to do something. How did I know that Samuel was about to do something? Mr. Fields would divert Samuel's attention by asking him a question or giving him a task, like connecting the iPad to Apple TV, so that he could not mess around. Talk about knowing your students! By being pro-active and making those little adjustments along the way, Mr. Fields was able to address behaviors before they even started.

On a side note, I learned later on that Samuel had been kicked out of school and had been in trouble with the law a number of times, but Samuel adored Mr. Fields and tries harder in his class than any other. While he still tries to goof around at any moment he can, he respects Mr. Fields because he knows he cares about him.

Utilizing these little adjustment techniques along the way that Ms. Bellow, Mr. Fields, and many more use in their classroom, will allow you to correct behaviors as they arise. Kids will mess up, it's in their DNA, and so as the adult, we need to be the one to address the issue immediately. Otherwise, we are left with looking back at the end of the year, or years later, thinking about the missed moments we had with a student.

What CAN you do? When you see a student who needs to be corrected, whether it is behaviorally, academically, or socially, it is our responsibility to address it immediately. If possible, do it without having to lose teaching time. Non-verbal cues, questioning, assigning tasks, or making eye contact can prevent or discourage behaviors before they even happen. If a behavior has already been done, do your best to address it immediately, even if it means saying, "I need to see you after class." This at least shows the student you have recognized the behavior and will deal with it soon. Like the pilot, your goal should be to make those small adjustments along the way so you can avoid going completely off course and can stay on target.

34.
You CAN ...
Teach Outside Your Comfort Zone

When I travel to schools, one of the services I offer is to model lessons. I feel it is helpful for teachers to see other educators teaching so that they may observe new approaches and ideas can be implemented. It is more personal when you can witness the teaching being done with your own students who you teach each day. Teachers have told me during the debriefing session that some of the most valuable moments are watching how I react to situations with students I do not know.

When I first started "taking over" a class and teaching the students for a 45-60 minute block, I had to learn how to establish rules, set my purpose, and teach my content in a short amount of time, all while being watched by handfuls of teachers noticing my every move. I loved the rush of the moment—entering a classroom of kids wondering who I was, what we were going to be doing, and figuring out if they were going to join me immediately or challenge me to win them over.

I modeled lessons in grades two through eight typically, with the occasional high school lesson thrown in there. Personally, it's where I have the most experience and feel the most comfortable. My personality fits that age range, and I believe I can get the most bang for my buck with them. About 95% of my lessons went well overall. Even the 5% that didn't go great still had potential; they just had some bumps that only I noticed.

But then there was the request I had always dreaded. The one request that I knew was going to come eventually, but I just made myself not think about it since I knew it was going to be painful to hear. The moment went something like this during a phone call with the curriculum coordinator:

"My kindergarten teachers are looking for some new ideas, and I wanted to see if you could model lessons for them so they could get some. I know it says grades two through eight, but I was hoping you could do kindergarten this once."

Crap.

If there is one thing I swore up and down as I entered my teaching career, is that I would never teach kindergarten. Frankly, they scare me. They're so little. They need to be told two hundred times what to do, and then still manage to screw it up. They pee on themselves, eat paste, and tattletale like it's their job.

To be fair, they are also loving, forgiving, and cute as a button, but so are puppies, and you don't see me running to teach them either. In other words, there are people far more fit than I to teach them.

On an aside, when you talk to a kindergarten teacher, they will often find every reason for why they will never teach the older kids. People just have their preferences!

With all that being said, I said yes, I would go outside my comfort zone and teach a math lesson to the kindergarteners. The next dilemma I had to conquer was to figure out what I was going to teach them. I am used to teaching function tables, order of operations, and geometric formulas, not counting up to ten.

I called upon a couple friends who teach kindergarten to give me a hand. With their help, I came up with two decent lessons, one involving 3-D shapes and the other involving combinations of ten. I was scheduled to teach two classes, so I decided I would try out both of these lessons since I would not be teaching kindergarten again anytime soon.

As the day approached, I went through the lesson a million times in my head—how I would establish my expectations, the hook into my lesson, and the appropriate pace. In my head, this was going to be perfect.

If only inside my head was reality. Reality hurts sometimes, and this was a perfect example of how sometimes lessons just don't go according to plan. I'll paint you a picture:

The first thing I did not realize was that while there were two lessons, each classroom would house two kindergarten classes, so I was looking at about forty-plus kids for each lesson. Even forty five-year-olds still take up a lot of space! Add about ten adults who were watching the lesson, and we were packed like a can of sardines, except the sardines sat about as still as a Mexican jumping bean.

I finally found a way to introduce myself and establish some expectations. As I was introducing myself, one of the children asked if I was the President. I said, "The President of what?" He said, "The United States." I said, "Do you know who the President of the USA is?" He replied, "Back Obaba" (not a typo). In typical sarcastic Mr. Dovico style, I said, "Yes, I am Back Obaba." That shut him up.

Dovico – 1, Kindergartners - 0

Eventually I explained how they were going to be detectives and search around the classroom for objects that looked like the shapes we had just watched a YouTube video on. It was actually a pretty good video; it's called "3-D Shapes I Know." I recommend it for those of you who are real kindergarten teachers!

I made a neat little detective sheet that the kids took around with them as they tiptoed around the room. When they found a 3-D shape that they knew, they were to draw a picture of the object and then write the name of it on the line. Great idea, right? Unless, of course, you realized that most five-year-olds insist on asking you how to spell every word. Oops, hadn't thought of that.

Dovico – 1, Kindergartners – 1

When we returned to our personal carpet square, for which World War III could have broken out when a child from another classroom tried sitting on a square that wasn't his, we shared what we found. Luckily, some of the teachers in the room were able to translate what the kids were sharing because I could not understand a word they were saying. It was as if we were speaking two different languages.

Dovico – 1, Kindergartners – 2

Nevertheless, I made them explain their paper, and even when the child I selected didn't want to speak, I gave them support and helped them by kneeling down and reciting their findings with them.

Dovico – 2, Kindergartners – 2

Before I knew it, my time had run up and I had made it through my first lesson with kindergarten. It wasn't pretty, but I made it. In the end, I am calling it a draw. I appreciate second chances, though, and I had one coming up in just a few minutes.

The second lesson seemed to go much better, even though, once again, I had over forty kids in there. The activity I did with combinations of ten was fun. To do it, the kids work in partners. The first partner has ten cubes in his hand. Then he says, "You can't see me," which means his partner has to close his eyes. By the way, I got that phrase from John Cena, a wrestler, which a number of the students picked up on. The first partner takes as many cubes as he wants away from the stack and puts them behind his back. Then he says, "You can see me," and the partner opens his eyes. He looks at the remaining cubes in front of him and has to determine how many cubes are behind his partner's back. If the team becomes good at it, they can start with a different amount of cubes than ten.

I originally thought that this activity was going to be a bit monotonous, but I quickly realized that five-year-olds love repetitiveness, so they ate this game up. The teachers enjoyed it, too, and said this was something that they were definitely going to play again.

To end, I threw a word problem at the students to see how well they truly understood the concepts. I told them that I was going to be having a birthday party for my five-year-old son (he was only one at the time, but they had no idea), and his two favorite colors were black and gold (just like daddy). I wanted to buy a combination of five black and gold balloons. I wanted to know how many different combinations of black and gold balloons I could have.

It's amazing how the second you put a word problem in front of students, all of the teaching and practice you just did goes out the window! Their little eyes got real nervous when I said we were going to solve it. They struggled for a while, but we worked together and solved it as a group. In the end, we had success and celebrated appropriately with an "AWWWESOME!" chant.

After the two lessons, I debriefed with the teachers from both rooms. I had a chance to reflect on what I thought about the two lessons, and the improvements I made my second time. I talked about better understanding the speed I needed to move with the kids, and the expectations that would work for them. They mentioned that they appreciated the high expectations and not allowing the kids to slip through the cracks just because they say, "I don't know." It was important for me to hear what these teachers were saying because they teach these kids each day and are experts at kindergarten, so I respected and appreciated their comments and feedback.

It was not easy teaching an age for which I am so unfamiliar. I have a deep respect for teachers who are asked to make giant switches in grade levels. It is not easy going to a grade level you are not comfortable or familiar with, even if for a couple hours.

If you have been teaching in the same grade or with the same population for a long time, I would encourage you to take that leap of faith and try another grade or demographic, even if for a year. It is nice seeing where the kids come from or where they are going from a first-hand perspective. When I began teaching at the Ron Clark Academy, being thrown in to teach sixth, seventh, and eighth graders was eye-opening for me, but I am so glad I did it because it has certainly made me a better teacher. As I go around to schools and model lessons in different grades and populations, it has given me a deeper appreciation for my fellow teachers and the work that they put in each day.

Don't be afraid of change. It is what makes us stronger, wiser, and more understanding.

What CAN you do? Challenge yourself to something outside of your comfort zone. To help you feel safe in a new environment, find expectations that work for you, so that no matter what the grade, the population, or the location, you have something consistent you are bringing with you. For example, when I go in to model lessons, or when I am with my own students, I have established three set rules that I carry with me and begin every lesson with:

1) *You are to maintain eye contact with the speaker at all times. No matter where in the classroom, your eyes are always on the speaker.*
2) *Maintain respect. This includes addressing me with "Yes, sir" or "No, sir," not having your hand up while someone else is speaking, and sitting up straight without your hand holding up your head (that drives me nuts).*
3) *When you are responding to an answer, you are to stand up and face the audience (classmates) and answer in a complete sentence.*

35.
You CAN ...
Learn Names

My first job was, in large part, thanks to Ms. Teresa Hewitt. Ms. Hewitt was the assistant principal at Vienna Elementary and a great supporter of me over the years. She, of course, did what assistant principals are expected to do (the three B's—books, bottoms, and buses—as one of my friends once told me), but she is known for so much more. In all my years, I have never met anyone who loved each and every child that came through the doors as much as her. There's more.

In what can only be deemed an extraordinary talent, Ms. Hewitt knew the first, middle, and last name of every child in that school. It doesn't stop there. She knew the name of that child's siblings, mom, dad, granddaddy, grandmamma, aunt, uncle, dog, cat, bird that died three years ago, and lizard that sleeps in the garage. It doesn't stop there. She knew where they lived, what bus they should be on, their birthdays, and any number of other factoids that can only be found through top-level security clearance. Her memory is astounding!

What I noticed, though, over my years working with Ms. Hewitt, is that it came in handy. When those children came off the bus in the morning, she was the first one to greet each one by name and give them a big hug and smile. When a child was having a bad day, she often knew what was wrong simply because she knew their families so well. In parent meetings, she was able to ask about older siblings and other family specifics that put angry or worried parents at ease. It was a talent and great lesson for me to learn as a young teacher.

The effort to learn everything about my students came in handy, as I was asked to do the commencement speech at the Vienna Elementary fifth-grade promotion ceremony years after I left the school. As I was walking down the familiar hallway to the auditorium to deliver the speech, I was stopped by the enthusiastic words, "Mr. Dovico!" As I looked up and saw the face that called my name, I immediately replied, "Elijah!" It was if I had seen him yesterday in my fifth-grade class, instead of nine years ago. Elijah was in my very first fifth-grade class and today his brother was graduating, which is why he was there. He had no idea I was going to be there, and clearly I had no idea he'd be there, so it was one of the most pleasant surprises I could have asked for. He said to me, "I can't believe you remember me." Truth be told, his face hasn't changed a bit, but it was my insistence on learning and imprinting the names of my students into my head that truly allowed me to remember Elijah that day. To add icing to the cake, his mom also had him wear his old "Dovico's Deacs" shirt that my class all received that year. I told him I couldn't believe he still had that (or that it still fit his now man-sized body)!

Elijah, nine years after I had him in fifth grade.

Many of the strategies and approaches that I learned from Ms. Hewitt and still use today, all came back to simply knowing names.

Learning names is something we do from the time we can talk and still do on a daily basis as we meet people. It is hard remembering names quickly when you have large or multiple classes, but it can be done with practice and utilizing some simple strategies. Here are some ideas:

1) Flashcards – Just like the good old days of studying for your chemistry exam, flashcards are still a great way to learn and practice material. With technology now, you can make flashcards using various websites and apps on a smartphone. One of my favorites is quizlet.com.

2) Repetition – Use the child's name each time that you address them. Instead of just saying, "Good morning," say "Good morning, Peter." When the child gives an answer, instead of verifying it with a "Yes", try inserting her name, "Yes, Aliyah, that's correct."

3) Placards – Each year I would start by making name tents (piece of paper folded into a pyramid) for each of my classes. Since I would receive three to five sets of kids a day, I would use different colored cardstock or construction paper for each class. All of the names for the students who sat at that desk would be in a stack, so at the end of class, the students were in charge of switching the placards over to the next class. This was easier than having the students' names flat on the desk because I could not always see them as I was teaching.

4) Name games – One of my favorite name games is acrostic poetry. Acrostic poems take the first letter of a word and write a line that starts with that letter. I would ask students to create an acrostic poem about them that describes their hobbies, personalities, family, or interesting things. As we shared with each other, this was a good time to make associations with the students based on their poem that would make it easier to remember their names. For instance, if Stephanie started out by saying "Soccer is my favorite sport," I would be able to associate soccer with her, and remember the "S" to link it to Stephanie.

Here is an acrostic poem to remember me by:

Aghast by anything messy my mother taught me to be

Driven by success and the desire to be the best

Awake at all hours thanks to my baby boy

Making education fun one classroom at a time

What CAN you do? People appreciate it when you refer to them by name. It shows that you remember them, and that is a great tool in the relationship building process. Take the time to learn the names of your students and parents in your class; imprint them in your memory. It will come in handy years down the road when you run into them in the grocery store and can still call them by name.

36.
You CAN ...
Pay It Forward

I went out to eat in Atlanta with my co-workers Kim and Joyce on a beautiful evening after finishing up work at school. We decided to eat outside since it was the perfect weather for it. As we were walking with the hostess to our seats, I noticed a gentleman seated at the bar with two large black and gold letters on his back: WF. In my mind, black and gold letters only mean one thing, Wake Forest!

I immediately gave him a tap on the back and said, "Wake Forest alum?" As he said he was, I introduced myself as an alumnus, as well, and we had a quick chitchat about how great of a school it is and how the current state of the basketball program makes us sick. We also noted how rare it is to run into Deacon alumni outside of North Carolina, so it was a pleasure seeing t-shirts without the word Georgia on it in Atlanta! (No offense to University of Georgia or Georgia Tech friends)

Kim, Joyce, and I had a nice meal together. As we asked for our check, the waitress said that Dave had already taken care of it for us and asked her to give us this:

Note from Dave, who committed an act of kindness.

This man who I had never met before tonight, and still only knew as a fellow alumnus from Wake Forest, had just paid for our entire dinner. This napkin said it all. Unfortunately, he had left before we could even say thank you. The three of us were speechless. And that's pretty hard to get three teachers at a loss for words!

This random act of kindness struck a nerve with all three of us, and when we were able to find words, the first thing out of all of our mouths was how we were going to pay this forward.

163

Dave had done something special. He directly impacted three people at that dinner table, but indirectly may affect dozens more by the time this is done. Who knows, maybe Dave was a benefactor of a random act of kindness, and he was just in the chain of paying it forward? Either way, Dave has changed how I look at people. As optimistic as it sounds, I really do believe in the good in people and that committing these acts of kindness can make a difference.

I framed that napkin and it sits in my office right next to my computer, so as I type this chapter, I am looking at it and reminded of my mission that Dave has set forth for me. I am committing myself to paying it forward, not just once, but as many times as I can so that goodness can continue to flow from one person to the next.

Whether you are a teacher, or not, reading this, commit yourself to finding ways to spread kindness around you. I suppose I always knew I should be doing that, but it wasn't until I was the recipient of a major act of kindness did it resonate with me and made me realize how impactful it can be.

I also learned that spreading kindness does not need to look a certain way or have a price tag or value on it. I know I often thought of kindness as helping those less fortunate or doing kind things for my students, and while that is still invaluable to me, I realized that it is simply about doing something kind for your fellow man, whomever they may be. From the richest to the poorest, oldest to the youngest, it is all about continuing this chain of goodness from one day to the next.

Just a couple of days after my experience, I found a way to commit my first pay it forward moment. I was driving up Georgia-400, which at that time was a toll road. Being no stranger to toll roads growing up in New Jersey, I know how annoying they can be. The tolls are only fifty cents, so I pulled out a five-dollar bill and explained to the cashier that this was going to be for me and the next nine people that came through. The lady at the window said that was very kind of me. I just smiled and said have a great day.

I don't know if the word invigorating accurately describes how energizing that feels when you know you have paid it forward. I have no idea who the next nine people in line were, nor will I ever meet them, but that is the whole point. It is about spreading this act of goodness with the hope that it makes people do the same.

Check this out! I'm a math person, so bear with me here as I do some computation. Starting from Dave, he directly affected three people with his act of kindness. If each of us spreads that to ten people, that would be thirty-three people affected. If each of those thirty people each affects ten people, we're up to three hundred thirty-three people. That kind of exponential growth blows my mind! I know math geeks feel me! And it all started because some guy wearing a Wake Forest t-shirt bought us a dinner.

In case you are somehow reading this book Dave, I would like to say, THANK YOU! And GO DEACS!

There is perhaps no one better at committing these random acts of kindness than Ron Clark. In my first year at his school, we received word that a school that had sent the entire staff through our educator training program had received a prestigious "Golden School" award for their excellent academic achievement by their state. When Ron heard about this, he asked Ms. Mosley to send the school a bouquet of golden flowers to congratulate them. How she found golden flowers (not yellow, but golden) is beyond me, but the school wrote us the kindest email and passed along pictures of the principal running through the halls showing each and every teacher what the Ron Clark Academy had sent them.

At the eighth-grade graduations, Ron is known for bringing in wonderful surprise guests to speak and perform at the ceremony. They have had Boyz II Men, Oprah, Master P, Inia.Arie, and many more. One of the biggest surprises of them all was Dr. Maya Angelou. She is a stirring individual and shared infinite words of wisdom with the 1,000 members of the audience. After her inspiring speech, Ron arranged for the staff to sneak backstage and get a quick picture with her. We were so excited and thankful, but realized afterwards Ron wasn't in the picture because he was still out on stage talking to the audience so we could take the picture. That selfless act shows the kindness he demonstrates so often without many even realizing it.

The Ron Clark Academy Staff with Dr. Maya Angelou.

What CAN you do? Opportunities to commit acts of kindness fall into our laps on a daily basis. Whether we choose to act upon it becomes the decision we must make. While it is impossible to take action on every opportunity, we must find ways to spread goodness. If you have been the recipient of a random act of kindness, you may be more inclined to pay it forward. If you have not, challenge yourself to be the first and set off your own chain of kind acts. While you may never come to realize your full reach, be confident that the goodness of people will come through, and the act of paying it forward will continue long after you began it.

37.
You CAN ...
Be Inside the Trenches

Our beliefs about school, education, and what it all should look like are formed and molded by our own experiences. From the time we are young, our thinking about what school is, is shaped by the teachers we are surrounded by and the children we are friends with. Rarely would you think that school looks differently in other places outside of your bubble. Our experiences also often translate into the value we hold and trust we have in the school system. These assumptions travel with us throughout our lives and are passed onto our children. It is only until we are able to understand the wide-spread variances in our education system before we can begin to realize the complicated and challenging task to fix education in America.

Growing up in a densely populated town in northern New Jersey, my vision of school included diverse ethnicities and races, religions and class systems. I had friends of every color and background, and that's just how it was. I didn't know any different.

When I began teaching in North Carolina in a suburb on the outskirts of a mid-sized city, my idea of what school looked like was edited. I taught a fairly homogeneous group of students, many of whom were from white Southern Baptist families.

Some years later, I would teach in an inner-city school where I was the only white face in my classroom. Once again, my idea of what school looked like altered.

In my role with the Ron Clark Academy, my idea of what school looks like has been twisted, turned, and expanded unlike ever before. Not only have I been able to observe, train, and work with thousands of teachers and hundreds of schools across the country, but I have been able to understand that education is a complex beast. There cannot be a single solution to fixing the problems in education because we are all coming into the discussion with such vast experiences and ideologies.

Can a school with 2,000 students say that they see education the same way as a school that sits in a town of 700 people? (I have been to both, and they do not.)

Can a school that sits in the middle of multimillion dollar mansions see education the same way as a school that sits next to a cotton field? (Once again, I have been to both, and they do not.)

Since people see education from different lenses, what is the answer to helping all students, everywhere? My experience in all of these different types of schools leads me to say that we must first open our minds. We have to accept that there is a world outside of our classroom, our town, our city; our personal experience in school does not mean that everyone had the same experience.

After we accept that disposition, we must find ways to help one another in tackling the challenges that we face in the classroom. I liken this to soldiers at war. Soldiers face unique challenges depending on where they are stationed and the conditions in which they are placed. But if you ever see soldiers addressing one another, they are always respectful of what each other went through because they know how difficult and honorable a job it is.

As educators, we, too, are inside the trenches each day. Our trenches include desks, bulletin boards, textbooks, computers, and the dozens of students that come in and out of them. We deal with angry parents, demands from central office, sick children, grading, lesson plans, and so much more. And while our children may look different or come from different backgrounds, we do share common challenges that bond us in our mission.

Life inside the trenches should be understood from many angles, and it is hopeful that in this book and other educational materials like it, you will be able to get ideas of what it can be like inside of schools in America. It is my desire that you open your mind to the fun, the craziness, the unexpected, the hurdles, and the emotions that educators enjoy each day.

About the Author

Adam Dovico is a National Board Certified Teacher, who has taught in public and private schools in North Carolina and Georgia for over a decade. He spent four years working as a teacher and school implementation specialist for the renowned Ron Clark Academy, where he traveled across the country, conducting professional development and on-site training to schools and districts for over ten thousand educators in twenty-seven states. He has also taught at the collegiate level as a clinical professor at Wake Forest University. Adam is married to his wife Jaclyn, and they have two sons, Ryder and Maddox.

STAY CONNECTED!

Follow Adam on Twitter @adamdovico and use #insidetrenches to discuss the book.

Like *Inside the Trenches* on Facebook at facebook.com/insidetrenches

Visit our website: www.insidetrenches.com

CPSIA information can be obtained
at www.ICGtesting.com
Printed in the USA
FSOW02n1138090916
24808FS

9 781499 570175